52 WEEKS
of PARENTING
WISDOM

Effective Strategies for
Raising Happy, Responsible Kids

MEG AKABAS

WITH SETH AKABAS · FOREWORD BY FRED A. BERNSTEIN

ISBN: 0615628656

ISBN-13: 9780615628653

Library of Congress Control Number: 2012906510

Parenting Solutions Press, New York, NY

Cover Design © Julie Metz & Heidi North/Julie Metz Ltd.

For:

*Shai, Tal, Shoshana, and Lev, who have encouraged
and inspired me, and who bring me joy every day*

and

*My parents who taught me so much
of what I know about parenting*

FOREWORD

Recently, we organized a birthday party for our energetic, seven-year-old twins. We took the boys and their friends to a minor league baseball game, where they could watch the action on the field, eat lunch, and play a few arcade games.

The boys behaved abysmally—they acted more like three-year-olds than children twice that age. When I mentioned this to a friend, he of-fered a sobering observation: the other children hadn't behaved any better. He was right, but it was small consolation. We, and the other parents, had set the bar for our children at a historic low.

You may be thinking, "They're seven-year-old boys. How can they be expected to be polite or stay in their seats for more than a few minutes?" If you *are* thinking that, imagine a time when seven-year-olds were expected to sit quietly in church and school, help raise infant and toddler siblings, and perform myriad other chores, some of which were crucial to their families' welfare.

It's not that children can't behave—it's just that we don't ask them to.

America is suffering an epidemic of low-expectations parenting. It's everywhere, from the popularity of gross-out books (which parents buy in the belief, reinforced by educators, that boys won't read unless they can read about farts) to the demand for snacks at every activity, lest children go an hour without access to food.

No wonder parents report—in several widely publicized surveys—that parenting is a drag. Parents expect very little of their kids these days, and that's exactly what they get.

Parenting is, and always has been, a self-fulfilling prophecy, and today's parents are setting themselves up for disappointment.

Worse, we aren't preparing our children for the world we're leaving them. I'm not talking about truly disadvantaged children, who face serious problems accessing education and jobs. I'm talking about kids who have opportunities but are not being asked to maximize them. We are preparing children to live in an affluent society in which their every need will be attended to, but that isn't the world they'll be inheriting.

Forget the global picture for a minute. If you're reading this book, you probably have more immediate concerns than the long-term economic outlook.

Short-term: How will you get through the day? Medium-term: How will your child ever make it through college without the "homework monitors" and tutors so many kids rely on, starting in kindergarten? And you're right to ask yourself those questions. But here's another question: Why have parents let this happen?

Here's Barack Obama's account of how his mother taught him English during his elementary school years in Indonesia: "Five days a week, she came into my room at four in the morning…fed me breakfast, and proceeded to teach me my English lessons for three hours before I left for school." Politics aside, Mr. Obama—who spent the rest of the day at a Catholic school where he was taught in Indonesian—went on to head the Harvard Law Review and write best-selling books in brilliantly evocative English.

Compare this to parents who think it's too much if their kids have ten minutes of homework. (Yes, there is a nationwide movement to eliminate homework because "it's stressful for children.") Barack Obama's mother gave him a gift—one that most American parents wouldn't have the guts to give their children.

I see it all around me. Here's what happened at a recent orientation for Hebrew school (which my children attend on Monday afternoons from 4:00 to 6:00 p.m.): The director presented a terrific report on the curriculum, which includes history, religion, culture, and language. But during the question-and-answer period that followed, parents didn't seem concerned about how the teachers could cover all of that in two hours a week. Here's what did concern them: snacks. "What kinds of snacks will you have for the kids?" one parent asked, adding, "My daughter can't go two hours without eating." There was a murmur of agreement among other parents and a few references to low blood sugar.

After that, the parents broke into smaller groups to meet with their kids' teachers. In my group, one mother said that after a long day at school, her son really couldn't be expected to do much reading or writing. She suggested that the children instead be asked to do physical things—like act out Bible stories. Other parents joined in and agreed that reading and writing were too much to ask of the children from 4:00 to 6:00 p.m.

Broccoli as Metaphor

Children need to eat healthy food. If they don't, it's because we, their parents, don't expect them to. It's not because we haven't perfected the techniques outlined in best-selling books about how to trick children into eating vegetables. According to that school of thought, the reason kids aren't eating well is that their parents aren't sufficiently sneaky.

Why should we have to trick them? In an article about children refusing to eat vegetables, a Houston psychologist, Susan Gardner, asked a sensible question: "Where are the parents of yesteryear who put out nutritious foods and expected their children would eat them?"

Children in past generations ate what was put in front of them because, if they didn't, they wouldn't get anything else. (Most children, for most of history, were lucky if they were given even one "choice" for dinner.)

So when people say, "My children won't eat vegetables," that's just another way of saying, "I've given my children the choice not to eat vegetables, and they took it." (Right? If there hadn't been a choice, they would have eaten vegetables. Unless you think your child would have starved him or herself to death—which some parents must fear is a real possibility.)

Broccoli is just the most obvious example of something children won't choose. Other examples include doing chores, being polite, and finishing difficult projects.

That's not to say children shouldn't have choices. In fact, they should have lots of choices; being allowed to make decisions helps them develop self-esteem and independence. Meg Akabas believes in giving children choices such as, "Do you want me to put on your shoes first, or your jacket?" (for little kids) and, "Which of *these* movies would you like to see tonight?" (for older kids). In those cases, you're happy with whichever one your child picks. In the realm of healthy food, "Do you want to eat broccoli or cauliflower tonight?" is a great choice because you're happy with either outcome. But, if you are like many parents, you may have asked your child, "Do you want to eat broccoli or macaroni?"

Sir Fartsalot

Not only do many parents have low expectations these days, educators also seem to be encouraging the don't-ask-too-much-of-the-children approach.

As *The Wall Street Journal* reported: In the view of many educators, "Boys shouldn't be asked to read anything that's difficult. A large number of teachers believe we must 'meet them where they are.'" "Just get 'em reading," one teacher counsels cheerily. "Worry about what they're reading later." Both driving (and benefiting from) the trend is a publisher, Penguin, which once used the slogan, "the library of every educated person." Its recent titles include "Sir Fartsalot Hunts the Booger."

One father I know, whose ten-year-old daughter goes to a private school in Manhattan, was told his daughter should be allowed to read only books that are "just right"—which the school defined as having no more than five unfamiliar words per page. "The five-words-per-page rule was formally elaborated for the kids at school by the librarian, the reading specialist, and homeroom teachers, empowering the children to reject any book that wasn't 'just right,'" the father recalled.

He wanted his daughter to read the *The Phantom Tollbooth*, which he says is a great book "precisely because it has as all sorts of odd usages, neologisms, and intentional juxtapositions of 'hard' words with their more common synonyms." But the choice didn't pass muster with the school. "I was told this book, my favorite when I was seven, was not 'just right.'"

Diapers as Metaphor

Another driver of low expectations is American consumerism, a culture in which buying the right product solves all problems.

Take pull-up diapers. The average age at which children are toilet trained has risen sharply, as companies like Procter & Gamble flood the market with ever-bigger diapers. The toilet-training philosophy these days, as one parenting expert wrote, is this: "Wait until your child is ready; don't force the issue of potty training. Just relax and use pull-ups."

Just relax? Children don't know that pull-ups cost money—lots of it—and stuff landfills to bursting. But parents know these things. And they should weigh the costs, as well as the long-term benefits for the child's social and psychological development, against their child's short-term comfort.

But in low-expectations parenting, there is no weighing—the child's desires are not just the beginning but also the end of the discussion. Why ask a child to confront a problem, if you can buy something to make it go away?

When "High" is "Low"

Even advocates who suggest setting high expectations for children seem to set low expectations. The Parenting Institute, which maintains a popular website for parents, gives six rules to get children to meet high expectations. Rule three is "make sure your child agrees that the expectation is both reasonable and achievable." The problem here is that waiting for children to agree that the expectation is reasonable means the child, once again, is in control.

Why Parents Have Low Expectations

So why do parents expect so little? It may have to do with the desire of parents to befriend their children and create a relationship of equals. The breakdown of traditional parenting roles means both father and mother are in a position to compete for the child's affection, which they make the mistake of doing by failing to set standards.

Then, too, parents are too busy and too distracted to ask much of their children—since setting rules and limits requires parents to follow through: turning off the TV, putting down the iPhone, and focusing on what the children are up to. But, to their credit, parents with low expectations probably just want their children to be happy. They are acting on the belief that giving them everything they want as children will make them happy as adults. If anything, the opposite is true.

Children, when they grow up, "will be happy sometimes, and unhappy other times—just like everyone else," said Laura Gold, a New York child, adolescent, and adult psychologist. "Our job as parents is *not* to try to ensure that our children feel happy all the time. It is to equip our children with the tools to manage the complexities and challenging situations that life inevitably presents, and the shifting feelings that accompany them." It follows, Gold says, "that if we are doing our job as parents right, our kids will sometimes be angry at us when we don't give them what they want. That's not just OK, it's actually good. It's important for kids to learn both that parents are in charge and that anger can safely and temporarily enter relationships. Conflict can arise, be talked about or simply tolerated, and eventually subside."

Indeed, giving your children everything they ask for isn't a form of love. It is, according to Meg Akabas, a form of neglect: the neglect of low expectations.

Akabas, an exceptional parent and parent-educator, can show you how to expect more from your children -- and get it.

- Fred A. Bernstein

TABLE OF CONTENTS

TABLE OF CONTENTS

INTRODUCTION

As a mother of four and a parenting educator, I know you may be overwhelmed—you feel you can't possibly do all the things you should to improve your parenting. You want to be sure you're doing the right things to raise happy kids, but you don't know where to start. This book provides a welcome solution: tackle one challenge at a time.

The idea of a book that encourages building skills in increments and layering them over time to create success is not new, but it has never been applied to parenting. Most parenting books are reference books that enable readers to find solutions to particular problems or questions. Got a problem with temper tantrums? Flip to the chapter on the "Terrible Twos" (a term I don't like for the reason you'll discover in my first chapter). Expecting a new addition to the family? Search in the index for "Sibling Rivalry." Other parenting books probe just one topic, such as how to get your child to sleep, and they typically provide exhaustive information on that single subject. Parents can easily become focused on the most seemingly pressing problem, while they overlook the full set of skills required to raise happy children.

I believe that every parent can be a better parent by working at the task slowly and steadily. *52 Weeks of Parenting Wisdom* is designed to take you on a journey, encourage you to think deeply about crucial parenting issues, and put practical strategies in place over the course of a year.

52 Weeks is meant to be read one chapter per week, and each chapter provides my most salient piece of advice on one specific topic. This method allows you to concentrate on making a single change that is attainable and effective, and you won't get overwhelmed and distracted by too much information. Set aside time to read an entry each week and (if applicable) discuss the philosophies presented with your parenting partner. At the end of each weekly entry, you'll find questions for reflection and a checklist of practical strategies to make improvements. Revisit this list throughout the week to remind yourself of the steps you need to take.

While I suggest reading the chapters in order (because they are generally arranged with fundamental topics at the beginning and more particular topics nearer the end), if a topic needs your urgent attention, you can find it in the contents and go to it right away.

If you feel you need to continue to work on a particular area until the methods become more routine, stick with it for another week or so. One or two chapters may not be relevant for you (e.g., the siblings section if you have one child), so you can skip those. The various pieces of my parenting philosophy are largely interdependent; you will be layering new skills on top of the ones you have put in place. When necessary, go back and refresh your memory about specific techniques.

52 Weeks is not a medical reference book. Nor is it a guide to producing smarter kids or improving their academic performance. I do think that if you follow the advice outlined in this book, you can instill in your kids a proper base for appreciating the joys of learning and self-discipline to succeed in school, but that benefit is just one of the many rewards that will emerge from kids who enjoy consistently sound parenting.

Finally, start this task as early as you can in the parenting journey. *52 Weeks* will best benefit parents of children from birth to age twelve. Where appropriate, some chapters feature sections that specifically apply the ideas to children in the outer spectrums of the target age range. These are entitled, "Starting Early" (for those with babies and young toddlers), and "As They Grow" (for those with children rapidly approaching the teen years).

Get ready to do some work to transform your parenting over the course of the coming year. Your children won't just be happier, they'll be respectful and sensitive to others, disciplined and self-motivated. They'll sleep well and let you sleep well, and they'll be a joy to have as family members and companions. You'll have happier children, and you'll be a happier parent.

WEEK 1

Watch Your Attitude

Self-fulfilling prophecies: Expect the worst of your kids and the worst is what you'll likely get

I heard it again just the other day: a parent bemoaning the inevitable behavior of a child going through a "phase." She complained that she couldn't get her son to drink the amount of milk recommended by his doctor. And then, she said it: "Teenagers—they never listen!"

How many times have you heard (or said) something similar? Although we all know not to "label" children (the smart one, the pretty one, the difficult one), we very easily fall into another trap—harboring (and even expressing) low expectations:

"She's about to hit the 'terrible twos.'"

"Boys will be boys."

"Kids these days…"

These statements all excuse unfavorable behavior with generalizations and predictions. And they become self-fulfilling prophecies. If you think all two-year olds go through a "terrible" phase, yours will. If you believe siblings can't get along, yours won't. If you're sure that all teens hate their parents, yours will.

It is not inevitable that children whine and throw tantrums throughout their young years. And they don't have to grow up to be sullen, rude teens either. It's all about expectations, truly. You can raise children without tolerating behaviors you find unacceptable. The trick is to start very early and be absolutely consistent about how you deal with those behaviors. Here are some points to keep in mind:

- Never (never!) reward undesirable behavior, especially whining. In the moment, giving in to a demanding, whining child or ignoring an inappropriate remark may be easier than doing the right thing. But consider the future, not just the moment.

- Always be sure a consequence (not punishment) follows unacceptable behavior (read about this distinction in Week 9: *No More Punishments*).

- Be very clear about expectations. That means be specific. Telling children that you expect them to "behave" doesn't really tell them anything. You must tell them *how* you expect them to behave.

- Model everything you expect from your child. For example, if you speak disrespectfully to your spouse or parents (even just once in a while), you can be sure that your child will speak disrespectfully to you.

Children won't continue a behavior that doesn't "work" for them. And children really do want to know what the boundaries are.

You will find very specific practical strategies in the weeks ahead, but before you begin to implement changes in how you parent, it will be very helpful to shift any attitudes that might work against your efforts. So I encourage you to replace those self-fulfilling prophecies with positive, clearly expressed goals and a parenting plan that will help you reach those goals.

QUESTIONS FOR REFLECTION

- What are some of my assumptions about how all children behave?

- What fears do I have about my child's development?

2

TO DO THIS WEEK

- Make a list of all the negative expectations you have about raising children in general and about your child in particular. Listen not just to what you say to others, but also to the thoughts you hear in your mind. Your list should include both present inevitabilities ("Whenever I leave my kids to play together, they end up in a screaming match with each other") and assumptions about the future ("Teens are alien creatures"). Give yourself a few days to develop your list, and stay alert for any defeatist attitudes that creep up. Use the "Expectations Worksheet" from the *52 Weeks of Parenting Wisdom* website (www.52WeeksofParentingWisdom.com) to record your list.

- On your worksheet, rewrite each negative assumption, turning it into your ideal scenario. Incorporate the values and hopes you have for your child/children. For example: "I'd like my children to play together peacefully and enjoy each other's company."

- As you read this book, note which chapters and parenting techniques will help you work toward each of these positive goals and record them on your worksheet.

WEEK 2

The Best Lecture Is a Good Example

Respect (Part I): Model it for your children

Your child's attitudes and behavior emerge from how *you* treat the people in your life.

The subject of respect for spouses or partners could be a topic for another book, but it plays such an important role in influencing children's behavior that I must write about it here in the context of parenting skills. We show regard for our spouses in many ways: through our words, facial expressions, body language, and actions. How you listen, empathize, support, show appreciation, and, perhaps most important, disagree, are demonstrated to your children during every moment you and your partner spend with your children (and this applies to divorced parents as well).

It's safe to say you should be hypervigilant about not:

- Yelling or snapping at each other

- Talking down to each other

- Making fun of each other except in a very good-natured way

- Undermining each other

You must set the highest standard for yourselves in this area because your children will miss nothing. If you slip (after all, no one is perfect), don't think no one noticed; your children should see you apologize, and you should explain to them why your behavior was unacceptable.

Almost as important as respect for your partner is respect for your parents (your kids' grandparents). Don't dream for a moment that kids are not acute observers of how you treat your parents, and don't delude yourself that your kids will not see the analogy—*my parents are to my grandparents as I am to my parents.* Roll your eyes at your parents, and you'll be graced with the same response from your kids. If you don't have time for your parents, don't be surprised when your kids don't have time for you.

I realize that many adults have difficult relationships with their parents, but even difficult relationships needn't keep you from modeling respect in front of your children. Sometimes, grandparents aren't in the picture, but modeling respect applies to all family members, including your siblings (your kids' aunts and uncles) and other important people in your lives.

The point isn't just making sure your kids treat you respectfully. It's about making sure they treat *everyone* respectfully. Do you acknowledge a doorman as you go in or out of a building? Do you thank the checkout person at your supermarket? Do you have patience and consideration for other drivers on the road? Kids will pick up on every interaction, so monitor your own behavior.

For strategies on how to treat children respectfully, see Week 6: *Those Who Give Respect, Get Respect.*

QUESTIONS FOR REFLECTION

- In what ways do I model respect for my children?

- In what areas do I need improvement?

- Which of my relationships provide strong examples of respect for my children?

TO DO THIS WEEK

- Recall and write down a short list of any recent incidences where you were not as respectful as you might have been towards your parenting partner, your own parents, or someone else in your life.

- Write next to each event what you could have done or said differently to provide a better model for your children.

- If you feel you and your partner's conduct in this area is lacking and that you can not change the behavior by yourselves, for the sake of your children, seek help.

WEEK 3

Don't Ask When You Mean to Tell

Firmness: Only ask a question if you're actually asking

Are you wondering why your children often don't listen to your directions? In Week 12: *Choices, Choices,* I explain why giving kids options as often as possible is a good idea. But here's a corollary: don't ask when you mean to tell.

I frequently hear parents *asking* their child to do something that is mandatory. I recently heard a mother, whose young child was precariously stepping out from the curb, call gently, "Laurie, can you not run into the street?" Hmm...did she really mean to offer a choice?

Parents sometimes use this kind of phrasing to avoid seeming bossy. A parent might say, "Kathy, will you clean up your room?" Kathy hears that she can answer yes or no. When she finds out that she doesn't have a choice, she's confused. *Telling* her to clean up her room would have worked better. (In addition, it's best to be as specific as possible. "Clean" is vague. Here is a better direction: "Kathy, please pick up your clothes from the floor and put them in the laundry, and then make your bed. Make sure you're done before we leave for your soccer game.")

I encourage you to notice whether you truly differentiate between asking and telling. Do you ask your baby, "Will you lie still for mommy?" when you're changing her diaper? If so, try (in a gentle, but firm voice), "Please lie still for mommy," or "Mommy needs you to lie still right now." Do you hear youself saying to your toddler, "Would you like to put on your shirt?" Substitute that with a kind but definitive "Please put on your shirt now." Also, be careful not to tag on an "OK?" at the end of your directions; "Brush your teeth before bed, OK?" is still a question.

Be clear with your child about what's optional and what's not. For example, if you know the temperature is below freezing, and you want your child to put on her jacket, don't offer a choice. If the weather outside is moderate, then you may want to offer a choice, by saying, "The temperature is a bit cool today, and you might want to put on your coat, but you could also wait until we are outside."

While these slight distinctions may seem trivial, remember that children are happiest and most cooperative when they live in a world that is predictable and secure. By being clear with your words to convey what you really mean, you are providing them with certainty and, therefore, reducing stress. The way we communicate with our children is really *that* powerful.

QUESTIONS FOR REFLECTION

- Do I feel guilty about telling my children to do so many things and end up *asking* them so that I seem less demanding?

- Have I fallen into the habit of using questions as my regular mode of speaking with my children?

- Do my children often ignore me when I *ask* them to do something?

TO DO THIS WEEK

- Be mindful of every instance when you are about to *ask* your child to do something or *tell* your child to do something. Determine in your own mind before you speak—is it a question or a direction—and then choose the appropriate wording.

WEEK  4

The Gift of Sleep

Sleep Habits: Help your child learn how to self-soothe

Asking a young child to go to sleep while you stay awake is basically asking him to experience a separation. Understand that, and you'll understand why some kids will do anything to avoid going to sleep.

Actually, it's possible for bedtime to serve as a quintessential family activity, a time of real closeness. In many families, however, bedtime is more of a battle. Helping your children develop good sleep habits is an important component of good parenting. Kids who are not well rested will be cranky, and kids who can't fall asleep by themselves will suffer stress that may manifest as anger and frustration at their parents.

Infants fall asleep by themselves naturally, but after approximately the age of four months, falling asleep alone is a skill that babies have to learn; like all other skills, the younger the age at which you start learning, the better. Many studies have shown that kids who do not learn how to fall asleep by themselves are likely to have trouble sleeping later in life.

You can't make kids want to go to sleep, and you can't *make* them learn how, but if you start a bedtime activity when kids are infants, keep to a regular schedule, and set clear boundaries—a rule against leaving the crib or bed, no food after bedtime, etc.—kids will accept the need to fall asleep and learn how to do it.

First, create a bedtime ritual. Try to perform activities, such as bath time and teeth brushing, in the same order each night. Perhaps you could sit with your child on your lap first and read a book or tell a story, and then put her into her crib or bed. Next, you could sing her three songs or recite a poem, such as Eugene Field's "Winkin', Blinkin' and Nod," give her a kiss and tell her you love her, say good night to each of her stuffed animals, turn on a quiet music CD, and leave the room.

These bedtime rituals should be ones that help your child feel drowsy. Here are two hints on bedtime rituals to induce sleepiness:

- Sing songs progressively more slowly and softly. Our favorites were folk songs, such as "Swing Low, Sweet Chariot," "Good Night, Irene," and "Kumbaya." You don't need a great voice to use this technique—kids don't care so much about singing ability.

- Tell your child to close her eyes and keep them closed, and refrain from singing unless she closes them. People can't fall asleep without first closing their eyes.

Whichever bedtime rituals you choose to do, just make sure you're consistent with them.

Also, whatever you do, make sure that the routine doesn't involve the child's being dependent on you to actually drop off to sleep. That means you shouldn't rock her to sleep, walk her around, lie down next to her, or sit in the room until she falls asleep (reassure her that you are right outside and will check on her often—then do). The reason for this is simple: If your child is dependent on you to fall asleep at bedtime, she will likely need the same kind of attention to fall back asleep in the middle of the night when she naturally awakens.

Second, to avoid middle-of-the-night issues, it's important to teach children to self-soothe. Perhaps she sucks on a pacifier, cuddles a stuffed animal, gently rocks herself, or rubs a piece of fabric (such as a baby blanket) against her cheek. Help your child try out different self-soothing techniques; for example, offer your baby a piece of fabric with your scent on it and gently stroke her face with it as you read to her on your lap, then let her hold it next to her face when you put her into her crib. In this way, you can help your child find a comforting routine that works to settle her down, but doesn't require your physical presence.

Be consistent in allowing her to fall asleep by herself. Your child might cry when you leave the room. Calmly tell her that you love her, but that it's time to sleep and that you are right outside and will come back and check on her. If your child is still crying after a reasonable interval, go back in and reassure her; you can briefly pat her, remind her that you're outside, etc., but don't pick her up, lie down with her, or bring her into your bed. Leave the room again, and if she continues to cry, make another appearance. (The first interval might be four minutes, the next six minutes, the next eight minutes, and so on. Use a timer in another room, if need be.) Continue this pattern until your child falls asleep, and use the same technique if she wakes up in the middle of the night.

This method, based on Richard Ferber's book *Solve Your Child's Sleep Problems,* really works and has successfully helped every parent I have advised. My husband and I used this method with all four of our kids, and we swear by it. It not only works, it works quickly if you are consistent in using it. It may take anywhere from one to three nights for your child to go to sleep without any crying (the less entrenched the bad sleep habits, the shorter the number of evenings), but once the method is learned, your child will fall asleep with no struggle. With this method, children learn to get themselves to sleep without unnecessary crutches.

Finally, if your child is no longer in a crib, establish the rule that she shouldn't get out of bed by herself. If she does, calmly and quietly carry or walk her back to bed without giving in to requests.

Starting Young

You can start to teach your child to self-soothe at around five or six months. You need to make sure that your baby is not hungry, but once she is fed, you'll want her to be able to fall asleep by herself in her crib.

If you think your child is waking in the middle of the night because of a medical reason, check with your doctor to make sure that there aren't other sleep issues occuring (such as apnea).

You should also be consistent about helping your child fall asleep at nap times. Take note of your baby's natural sleep pattern and begin to schedule naps to fit the pattern, and then apply the same techniques described above.

As They Grow

This process will work for older children if modified appropriately. If you have a child nearing teen years who still needs help falling asleep, you can improve sleep habits, but only by being consistent in teaching your child to self-soothe, and by not assisting with the usual associations that your child has come to need.

At any age, the advantage of having children who can sleep through the night unassisted is that they develop good sleep habits that will stay with them, *everybody* in the household gets a better night's sleep, and, as a parent, you know when your child cries in the middle of the night that something is truly wrong (such as an ear infection). If you have a child who can self-soothe, you needn't worry about the "boy who cried wolf."

We taught all four of our children to soothe themselves to sleep when they were babies (as soon as they no longer needed night-time feedings), and they are all excellent sleepers as teenagers and adults. When you help your children achieve sleep independently, you are giving them a gift. And you'll get a better night's sleep, too.

"When you help your children achieve sleep independently through the ability to self-soothe, you are giving them a gift!"

QUESTIONS FOR REFLECTION

- Is bedtime a pleasant time for our family or a dreaded misadventure? At what stage of the process do we get tripped up?

- Are my children able to fall asleep without a grown-up's presence?

- Do my children call or come to me for assistance in the middle of the night when they are not sick?

TO DO THIS WEEK

- Create a bedtime routine (twenty to forty minutes for a small child, and less time if you're starting with an older child) that you can implement on a consistent basis. Put this routine down on paper and allot approximate times for each step.

- After implementing the routine, make sure your child stays in bed. If she gets out, bring her back consistently without caving in to requests.

- Help your child develop self-soothing techniques. Write down your reasons for teaching your child good sleep habits, and keep those reasons at the forefront of your mind as you begin to implement a bedtime routine, which might require you to endure some crying and protests, but which will result in your child's falling asleep by herself. Offer your child various self-soothing options to see what helps her relax. If necessary, return to the room at intervals to reassure her (or, if your child is older and emerges from the bed, bring her quickly and quietly back to bed without engaging her). Repeat the ritual for middle-of-the-night awakenings, if necessary. Your child may show tenacity in resisting your efforts, but if you are absolutely consistent (remember your reasons), she will learn to self-soothe.

WEEK 5

Sense and Sensitivity

Sensitivity: Teach children how to be wonderful family members and friends

Developing sensitivity to others' thoughts and feelings is one of the most important skills you can teach your children. While children are born egocentric, they gain awareness of others' individuality in the second half of their first year. Research shows that they can even make moral decisions at this stage (for example, children this age will almost uniformly choose to play with a puppet that is shown "helping" rather than "hindering" other puppets).

Kids won't fully understand the need for respect or be able to completely embrace sensitivity toward others until about the age of four or five. However, they can certainly start to learn and begin to form good habits in these areas through guidelines that you set long before they understand the underlying concepts.

Here's an example: When a young child wins a game, he will often exult and proclaim, "I won, I won! I beat you. I won!" In our family, we've always had a rule that the winner can say, "I won" only once. We had to repeat this rule many times to our children when they were young to override the natural tendency to repeat the phrase, but gradually refraining

19

from boasting became habit for them. They each just accepted the rule, at first probably without understanding the reasons behind it. Then, as we explained and explained, and they felt what it was like to be on the receiving end of insensitivity from others, they came to understand that saying, "I won" more than once shows insensitivity to how the loser might be feeling. This is a classic case in which adopting the right behavior early on sets the stage for understanding later.

As kids grow, you'll see many other examples of minor insensitivity, which you should nip in the bud. When one child shows another child his work, the other child might say, "That's easy," or "I did that a long time ago." We would not allow our children to make these statements (and, if they did, they had to apologize), and we imposed the same standard on their friends when they came to play in our home. Again, we would stop the behavior with an explanation they may not have understood at first. Eventually, though, they came to understand that belittling or minimizing someone else's work or effort is uncaring and shows a lack of respect.

When you observe a person saying something unkind to another, point it out to your kids and explain why the statement was insensitive. (Best to do this as soon as possible, while the words that were spoken are still fresh in everyone's mind, but naturally not in front of the person who is behaving thoughtlessly.) Also, discuss what other words the person who was speaking insensitively could have used instead.

Kids can also tell you what happened in school or at playdates—generally a prodigious source for examples of insensitivity. (Asking whether kids' daily interactions included any insensitivity is like asking if politicians ever exaggerate.) Our children would relate an insensitive statement, or report that a friend was upset about something someone said. Such examples were opportunities to discuss what was said as if we'd all witnessed it. Overall, we tried to make clear that we don't tolerate an uncaring attitude for the same reason we don't allow hitting or slapping—words can hurt.

As with all behaviors and principles that you want your children to learn, you must be absolutely consistent. Don't let infractions slip by under the guise of "kids will be kids." Kids can be sensitive kids *if they are taught* to be sensitive.

If you preach sensitivity, you will often have to be ready to respond to your child's complaints about the insensitivity of others. What we say to our children goes something like this: "Usually when a kid says something insensitive, *he* has a problem that he's trying to overcome. If your friend tells you that what you accomplished is easy, he probably said that because *he* feels bad about something. He has doubts that he can do what you do, so he builds himself up to make himself seem better than you."

A lot of juvenile insensitivity—"you're stupid," "you don't know what you're talking about," etc.—may well stem from such insecurities. Your child will undoubtedly have a lot of questions about that explanation, but talking about it will give him a context for others' insensitivity.

When you teach your children to be sensitive about how their words and actions affect others, you are giving them a critical life skill, and they will realize great rewards in terms of family harmony and the development of sound relationships. Parents who seize opportunities to foster sensitivity (as well as model it) when their children are young will reap huge benefits, among them: children who have fortitude, are kind, and are well-liked.

QUESTIONS FOR REFLECTION

- In what ways do I model sensitivity for my children?

- Do I talk to my children about what it means to be sensitive to others and about the power of words?

- What rules do I have to guide my children toward sensitive behavior?

TO DO THIS WEEK

- Set sensitivity guidelines with your children, such as "We only use kind words," and "We are careful not to put others down with our actions and words."

- If you notice that your child is employing insensitive words or actions, immediately bring it to his attention, have him apologize to the person whose feelings he might have hurt, and provide him with alternative language to use.

- Call your children's attention to others being sensitive. When you witness your children being sensitive, offer heaps of praise.

WEEK 6

Those Who Give Respect, Get Respect

Respect (Part II): Treat your children respectfully with both actions and words

Some two thousand years ago, the philosopher Simon Ben Zoma, posed the question, "Who gets respect?" and provided the answer, "The one who gives respect." Applied to parenting, this adage pretty much says it all.

You can show respect for your children in various ways, and many of them are covered in other chapters: demonstrating respect by setting clear expectations (Week 8), being consistent (Week 7), providing logical, not random consequences (Week 9), making a clear distinction between instructions and questions (Week 3), speaking to children in an appropriate tone and level of maturity (Weeks 17 and 23), paying attention to them (Week 19), treating them as individuals (Week 21), showing them common courtesy (Week 28), and asking for their input when appropriate (Weeks 31, 35, and 43). As you can see, many of the strategies in this book are based firmly on the concept of treating children with respect.

"Respect" is defined by Webster's as "due regard for the feelings, wishes, or rights of others." When I ask parenting workshop attendees what they think respect means, they readily come up with on-target words such as "consideration," or "thoughtfulness," "treatment with kindness and care, and without offense," and "treating others the way you want to be treated."

But do we always treat our children with respect? The answer is no, at least in many instances. For example, parents often talk about children in their presence as if they aren't even there. Another mistake we make is labeling our children. Both of these common practices are offensive to children in the same way they are offensive to adults, yet parents do them all the time. Labeling, in particular, calls into question our respect for children as individuals with many dimensions.

Other forms of disrespect for children often stem from impatience. It is absolutely necessary to deal patiently with your children when they speak to you. Express empathy with complaints (not whining) and feelings, pay careful attention to their questions, and explain your answers fully. Some of our lack of respect comes from arrogance. It's important to acknowledge when you've made a mistake or you don't know something. And, don't assume that you always know more than your children—kids are smarter than we think.

Finally, honor your children's taste. Words such as "stupid," "silly," "disgusting," "ugly," or "crazy" have no place in the language you use to describe your opinions about what your child likes or cares about. For example, if your child is obsessed with a new song by Katy Perry and you can't quite appreciate it, don't say it's "garbage," but instead try, "It has a catchy rhythm. It's not really my kind of music, but I can see why you like it."

As with all of the strategies in this book, you must be absolutely attentive to your own behavior. If you are even a "little" disrespectful to your children, you will experience that disrespect tenfold in return.

QUESTIONS FOR REFLECTION

- Do I sometimes talk about my child to other grown-ups when my child is within earshot?

- Do I ever label my child, either negatively (he's the messy one) or positively (she's the athlete of the family)?

- Do I show patience when my children ask questions that may seem silly to me or annoy me?

- Am I able to admit to my children when I have made a mistake or don't know something?

- Do I show proper consideration for my children's taste in music, clothes, and entertainment?

TO DO THIS WEEK

- If you have a baby, start practicing respect now. When you get in the habit of talking about your baby in front of him, you are more likely to continue doing so once he can understand you.

- If your children are older, don't wait a moment longer to demonstrate respectful behavior. Examine your own actions under a microscope, and pause before you speak to ensure you're not saying something that would be disrespectful to an adult.

- Work to develop patience. When your child asks her fiftieth question of the day, take a deep breath and remember that children are curious and deserve validation as they search for answers.

- Practice being respectful of your children's tastes. Remember that you don't have to agree with their preferences; as long as they don't violate your family's values, your children have a right to their own likes and dislikes.

- Ask yourself repeatedly at different junctures during the day: "Is this the way I would want my children to treat *me*?"

WEEK  7

Say What You Mean and Mean What You Say

Consistency: Provide security for your child by following through

Insecurity—particularly not knowing what is going to happen—is stressful for babies and children, and stress has all kinds of negative consequences. Unfortunately, parents unknowingly cause feelings of insecurity in their own children when their words and actions aren't consistent.

> "Parents unknowingly cause feelings of insecurity in their own children when their words and actions aren't consistent."

This phenomena can be understood by looking in an unexpected place: modern game theory. Game theory analyzes situations in which the actors do not have complete knowledge. It was developed in part to supplement classical economic theory, which assumes that all participants in the economy have complete knowledge. Game theory also offers insights into how to deal with other situations composed of imperfect knowledge, such as the Cold War nuclear confrontation.

Game theory situations are, in fact, stressful. People old enough to remember the nuclear war drills of the 1960s, and the arms race days of the 1970s and '80s, know this instinctively. Children, like adults, hate uncertainty and the stress that it breeds. They don't want to guess what is expected of them. They truly want to be told what to do, at least until they reach adolescence.

Parental rules and disciplinary plans will result in uncertainty and stress unless children are quite clear about what those rules and plans entail. Infants, toddlers, and young children have imperfect information about their parents' capabilities and intentions. This imperfect information makes children seem irrational at times, though they are not. When a parent gives an instruction, the rational child obeys, *but only if the child knows that her parents mean what they say.* A rule will be effective only if you give your kids perfect knowledge, which means that you always explain clearly, implement the consequences, and apply appropriate follow through. When parents are crystal clear about instructions and follow through every time, kids will nearly always do the right thing.

Every time a parent annouces a decision or gives an instruction and then does not follow through, the parent creates doubt and uncertainty for the child. The child, with merely a nascent understanding of human behavior, already has a handicap in understanding what actions constitutes doing the right thing (i.e., following the parent's directions and decisions). When a parent introduces even more doubt, the child is thus placed in a constant game theory situation. Moreover, when a parent is inconsistent, even his or her own sophisticated understanding of people may be inadequate, and that parent is thrown into greater doubt about how the child will respond. If children and parents are in doubt about what each will do, the interaction—according to the game theory—is likely to be volatile.

"Mean what you say" doesn't just apply to discipline; it also applies to what you tell your child you're going to do. It's easy to make promises to our children to appease them in the moment, but one loses credibility and trust if one fails to follow through. So, if you tell your child what you are going to do, even if it's seemingly minor, such as researching an answer to a question as soon as you return home, make sure that you do it. These small promises add up, and your child will learn whether you are someone he can count on or not. Reliability will go a long way toward fostering a sense of security and happiness in your children.

QUESTIONS FOR REFLECTION

- What disciplinary threats do I make and not follow through?

- Do I say things like, "I'm going to count to three," but then, after I count to three, do nothing?

- Do I make promises to my children and then forget to keep those promises?

TO DO THIS WEEK

- Watch your words. Before you speak, take a moment to think about what you are about to convey to your child and whether you really mean it.

- Consistently enforce all directions and decisions.

- This week, to get into the habit, whenever you tell to your child you are going to do something with/for him, write it down. Check your list often. This will help you follow through and will highlight which promises you might be making that you can't or don't intend to keep.

WEEK  8

Great Expectations

Be crystal clear with your kids about desired behavior

Imagine you're taking your daughter to a birthday party. Do you assume that she is going to know how to behave? Why not *tell* your child on the way to the party what behavior is expected? And why not be specific? Saying something like: "I expect you to behave at Charlie's birthday party" is not enough. It's a start, but "behave" how?

Instead, try to anticipate what your child might need to know about how to act at the party. For example, discuss the fact that she will participate in activities and games and that you expect her to listen carefully to the instructions given by the grown-up in charge, follow the rules and directions that are given, take turns in activities that require turns, and not make any fuss if she doesn't win. Talk about what manners to use when the cake is served. Talk about the fact that the birthday child will get many presents and that the guests may or may not get a gift bag when they leave. You might ask your child what she will say when she wants more cake, what she should do if she doesn't like the game being played, what she should say if she doesn't like the food that's served, or how she will react if she wins (or loses) a game.

You'd be amazed how many instances of misbehavior, bad discipline, and generally unpleasant interactions between parents and children emerge from the child's simple ignorance of what she is supposed to do. Children must be told (and then reminded, as many times as it takes) how you expect them to behave.

This rule applies to both specific actions (like how to say "hello" when a guest comes to visit) as well as to broad principles, like respect, self-control, and sensitivity (discussed at length in other chapters), and in all situations (going to a party, going on a playdate, visiting grandparents, being dropped off at school, going to bed). Talk to your children about what you expect of them early and often.

I frequently see parents missing this basic step. They simply don't convey in words what limits and expectations are in place until the the child does something "wrong," or when they do talk about behavior, they are not specific enough. Often, if they've talked about it once, they mistakenly assume that their child was listening and paying attention, understood completely what was conveyed, and will forever remember the important lesson.

Long before an event, think about what scenarios you will need to review with your child beforehand. If the event is one your child has attended before, recall prior problems; if the event will be your child's first time in that particular situation, think about his or her personality, and try to anticipate potential scenarios that might arise. Make a mental (or, better, a written) list of what issues you should review with your child, and discuss each item on the list by asking your child what to do and responding to her answer.

The easiest way to help a child understand what you are telling her is to describe situations and then ask her what she should do. "Sarah, what should you do if you are served cake with vanilla icing, since you don't like vanilla icing?" "David, what will you do if you are playing musical chairs and you are the first one out?"

Kids, like any of us, respond best to the call to a higher standard. They need to know not only what they *can't* do; they also need to know what they *should do*—in other words, the behavior to which they should aspire. Being clear with your children *proactively* will help you avoid all sorts of problems in the moment.

> "Kids need to know not only what they can't do; they also need to know what they should do."

QUESTIONS FOR REFLECTION

- In what recent siutations have I been embarrassed by my children's behavior?

- Could the embarrassing behavior have been prevented if I had briefed my children in advance?

TO DO THIS WEEK

- Think of two or three upcoming social situations that might be challenging for your child.

- For each situation, brainstorm about the many potential pitfalls that might arise.

- Envision what kind of behavior would replace each of the problematic behaviors on your list.

- Before each event, have a focused discussion with your child about expectations. For example, when you are talking to your children about visiting their grandparents, explain in advance what they cannot do (jump on the couch, throw balls in the hallway), but, at the same time, tell them what they must do (for example: tell grandma what you did today). Then ask hypothetical question, such as "What could you do if you see grandma has trouble carrying the dishes to the table?" "What if you get bored of sitting at the dinner table?" See how many potential problems you can head off and what good behavior you can inspire using this method.

WEEK 9

No More "Punishments"

Consequences: How they are different from punishments—and more effective

"**I** don't know how to get my children to listen to me!"

I hear that complaint all the time from parents. Most parents use punishments to try to motivate their children to behave well. But punishment is unnecessary, and it can breed resentment, anger, and frustration. Believe it or not, it's often counterproductive.

Instead of punishments that make no sense to a child, provide *logical consequences* for negative behavior. It is crucial to think of a consequence that relates to the behavior and then consistently follow through to create an environment of stability. This method works extremely well because the child sees a direct cause and effect, not random responses to her behavior.

Let's say your child has made a mess in the playroom, even though you've told her many times to put away one toy before she plays with another. Instead of imposing a punishment, such as saying, "You can't watch your TV show today," try this: Wait until your child asks to play a game or do an activity with you. As soon as she does, say, "I'd love to, but look how you've left the playroom. You know the rule—we have to clean up from one activity before we start the next. You need to put away your toys before we can play your game."

This principle may seem simple (and it is), but often, when we're in the moment, we don't think of these obvious ways of getting our children to comply. The same logic applies even to egregious misbehavior. An example: Say your three-year-old is kicking your two-year-old under the table during dinner. You could yell at her, but instead, you should firmly and calmly tell her to stop immediately and apologize to her brother and give him a hug. If she refuses, remove her from her chair and separate her from the family meal. The message is that she cannot sit at the table with everyone else if she can't control herself physically. At the next meal, remind her that she has a chance to sit with the family again as long as she controls her legs.

Another example: You've told your daughter to brush her teeth and put on her pajamas for bed, but she ignores you and continues to play with her dolls, insisting she just needs ten more minutes. You might be tempted to give her a lecture about how she needs to listen to you, and, because she didn't, she can't go to her friend's house the next day. A more logical and effective way to handle the situation would be to simply tell your daughter that because she took so long to follow your directions there isn't time for stories or singing before bed (or whatever it is that she cares about in the bedtime ritual). After all, this is a real-world consequence for procrastination.

The distinction between consequences and punishments may seem slight (in fact sometimes it is just in your wording), but the difference is huge in how effectively consequences influence your children to learn proper behavior. Consistently coming up with consequences instead of punishments takes practice, but you will improve the more you do it. Sometimes, when no logical consequence comes to mind, have your child sit alone with nothing to engage her for a set amount of time (see Week 11: *Tweaking Time-Outs*). Do not present this "time-out" as a punishment. Rather, introduce it as a *consequence* of the misbehavior, and let your child know she must think about what she did wrong.

When you break the habit of "punishments" and begin to easily come up with the appropriate logical consequences, you'll start to see your children follow your directions the first time you tell them something. Instead of harboring resentment over punishments, they will understand that their own undesirable behavior leads directly to undesirable results.

QUESTIONS FOR REFLECTION

- Do I threaten/use "punishments" when my child misbehaves? The last time I threatened a punishment, what might have been a logical consequence?

- Do I often have trouble figuring out what to do to get my child to behave the way I want?

- Which punishments do I resort to that are unrelated to the offense?

TO DO THIS WEEK

- Think about unacceptable behavior that you've been trying to remedy, and brainstorm how you might apply a logical consequence the next time it occurs.

- Whenever you are faced with an inappropriate action or inaction from your child, take a moment to think about what might be the logical consequence that follows your child's behavior and apply it. Do not negotiate or give in once you have decided on a consequence.

- Brainstorm with your parenting partner or another caregiver about logical consequences for situations that are likely to come up.

WEEK  10

Limits with Love

Boundaries: Provide security (and love) by setting and adhering to them

Kids need boundaries—we've all heard it and know it's true. It falls to you as a parent to define and impose your family's boundaries, which isn't as hard as it sounds.

First and foremost, you must be clear in your own mind about what the boundaries are. This may seem obvious, but most parents don't put enough advance thought into this crucial step. Constantly making rules on the fly will get you in trouble, so take time to consider in advance what you will and won't allow.

Once you're clear in your own mind about boundaries, next you must clearly communicate with your kids. For example, if you need a child to stop hitting his little brother, don't tell him to "stop bothering his brother," because that is a demand that may be too vague even for a well-meaning child to follow. Instead, say exactly what is and isn't tolerated. (In our family, the rule was no touching, except for hugs and other affectionate contact.)

Kids may not initially believe you when you explain a rule, and might think, "OK, that's what she says, but what's the *real* rule?" As parents, we inadvertantly encourage that kind of thinking by being unclear about what really matters. We impose "rules" like "don't bother me when I'm watching TV," which is more of a vague request or reprimand than a clear rule. It's necessary to distinguish between "try not to make a mess," and "you may not throw food against the wall." Only the latter provides the necessary guidance.

Once you've established a boundary, be firm! If your children don't comply, you must deliver a consequence (refer back to Week 9 if necessary). Kids want and need to know what limits are being set regarding their behavior. They will keep testing and pushing on the boundaries until they determine what the "real" rules are—and that means you must be clear and consistent.

Starting Early

It's important to begin setting boundaries early on. I suggest that parents start with a few clear boundaries around the time a baby is four to six months old. Possibilities include: no grabbing nearby bottles of powder and lotion during changing; no touching electrical appliances, etc.

As They Grow

Some rules will always stay in place, but many boundaries will evolve as your child grows older. For example, bedtimes change, as do expectations about how long a child might be required to sit at the table when guests are present. The key to adjusting rules is to initiate the changes gradually, and to clearly communicate the changes (and the reasons for the changes) to your children.

QUESTIONS FOR REFLECTION

- Am I clear *myself* about what is acceptable and not acceptable?

- Am I clear with my children about acceptable and unacceptable behavior? Do I impose boundaries consistently?

- If asked, would my children say that they know the family rules?

TO DO THIS WEEK

- Take some time to consider cases in which you have been clear or vague. Clarify the latter rules in your own mind. You may find that putting the specifics in writing is helpful.

- Review with your children any rules that were previously unclear. You may want to make a poster listing the basic house rules.

- Remember that every time you enforce a rule, you are showing your child love by giving her security. Work on making sure that what you *say* is a rule is *actually* a rule.

WEEK  11

Tweaking "Time-Outs"

Time-Outs: They can be effective if used sparingly and only as a "consequence"

Because you can't always generate just the right consequence immediately, it might be necessary to have your child sit alone for a set amount of time; this can sometimes be the best response to misbehavior. In our home, we never labeled this a "time-out," and the way I suggest implementing this consequence results in subtle differences from how most people define time-outs.

Here's how it works: When your child misbehaves, you carry him (or if he is older lead him by the hand) to a chair (or other designated spot) where you can keep an eye on him, but where he isn't in the center of the action. It's best if the chair is not in the child's bedroom because his bedroom should be a place of safety and comfort. Take him to the chair immediately when the infraction takes place. If you think of a better, logical consequence later, you can add it. Any delay or warning only enforces and encourages the misbehavior.

Firmly tell your child he needs to sit in the chair for a set amount of time (you can use a timer, and the number of minutes equal to his age works well) and think about what he has done wrong. If your child gets up from the chair, just calmly carry him back without engaging in conversation, and show him that you are starting the timer again. Once the time is up, the child may leave the chair once he has explained what he has done wrong and apologized. If he needs a hint, or even a full description, you should provide it, but make sure he relates it back to you. If he has hurt another person, he needs to apologize to that person and give him or her a hug.

With a very young child, you don't need to take any further action than carrying him to the chair and having him tell what he did wrong after the set time is up. For older children, who should be more responsible for controlling their behavior, sometimes you do have to take more action. At this point, the consequence chair has another great benefit; it gives you a chance to figure out what you're going to do next. It helps you avoid committing too hastily to any one course, and you have a chance to think about the misbehavior and arrive at an additional negative consequence that logically follows from the misbehavior. For example, if a child said some nasty words to a sibling, then you might make him apologize and give the sibling a big hug. If a child has thrown his food on the floor, he should help clean it up.

When you have your child in the chair, do not pay any attention to him except to keep him from leaving the chair. When he has calmed down and is ready to listen and talk about what he did wrong, make sure he conveys his misbehavior (e.g., "I threw a toy at my brother") keeping him in the chair until he does so. Sometimes he may not even know exactly what he did wrong, or is just too upset to think of it. At these times, you can give helpful hints or explain it and then have him repeat it.

If you haven't implemented this strategy when children are young it can take longer since, as kids grow older, their behavior patterns become more ingrained. You may have to be patient and re-start the timer if your child leaves the chair, but never interact with the child—except to discuss the misbehavior—while he is in the chair. Any activity or interaction in such a situation other than discussing the misbehavior would be a reward rather than a consequence for the misbehavior (i.e., it will show the child that he can get attention by misbehaving).

Once your child understands and says what he did wrong, always give him a big, warm hug and tell him that you love him. This final affirmation of your love shows your child that the temporary consequences that flow from misbehavior won't deprive him of your love.

This method is slightly different from a "time-out" in that, as the name implies, "time-out" is a more passive means of discipline than my method. A "time-out" is generally just a break from misbehavior in an effort to allow the child to naturally regain control. This could also be viewed by the child as a punishment. My strategy employs instructional and interactive components that respectfully teach the child what he did wrong and uses the principle of cognitive dissonance to help establish his inclination to behave properly. (See Week 24: *Belief Follows Behavior.*)

Starting Early

You can use this method with young children as soon as they can understand adverse consequences and can speak. It's best to start early for obvious reasons (you can't physically make a sixteen-year-old sit in a chair). If you start when your child is a toddler, you will not need to use the "consequence chair" often, because, as a result of being absolutely consistent and clear about what is expected in the first place, children quickly make acceptable behavior the norm.

QUESTIONS FOR REFLECTION

- What do I do when I can't figure out a logical consequence for misbehavior?

- Have I tried time-outs, but found they don't have the desired effect?

TO DO THIS WEEK

- Decide on a spot (a chair, the bottom step of a staircase, a stool on a corner) that will serve as a place where your child can sit to think if he misbehaves and there is no obvious consequence.

- Decide on a specific period of time that will be appropriate for your child. As suggested above, the number of minutes equal to your child's age works well. Have some sort of device available to keep time.

- When your child behaves inappropriately and no obvious, immediate consequence comes to mind, implement the technique described above. Do not hesitate, make threats, give second chances, or waver. Follow through with the entire process from start to finish and apply it consistently.

WEEK  12

Choices, Choices!

Cooperation: Take control by giving options

Parents often tell me that they have a terrible time with simple, daily activities, such as dressing their kids. Getting dressed often turns into a struggle when children resist or ignore directions.

Why do children make things difficult? In many cases, they are trying to obtain some control in a world where they perceive that they are always being told what to do. They can feel powerless and frustrated by the fact that they have little say in what happens to them in the course of a day. The answer? Give them back some of that power.

When you are frustrated by your children's determination to be uncooperative, consider this: the more choices you give your children about things they can control, the easier you will win cooperation when you need it. The solution, however, isn't to let your child just have her way. Rather, you can deliberately and proactively give your child choices in situations that are appropriate—and you end up happy with whatever option the child selects.

> "The more choices you give your children about things they can control, the easier you will win cooperation when you need it."

With toddlers, I suggest providing many, many small choices in the course of a day:

- Would you like to use the blue cup or the red cup?

- Do you want me to tie your shoes or zip your jacket first?

- Would you like to read this book or that book?

- Which do you think we should use to wash your feet, the sponge or the washcloth?

You may wonder why your child would care about these seemingly insignificant options, but (trust me) having the opportunity to make all of these small decisions will give your child a feeling of control.

You can begin giving choices to a baby once she is able to point by letting her choose between two stuffed animals to take in the car. With older children, find as many opportunities as possible to let them state their preferences. For example, let them choose which sports activity they'd like to pursue, the order in which they complete homework assignments after school, whether they'd like to have dessert right after dinner or an hour later as a fun family break, or which video you will watch together on Saturday night. Then, if your child resists a situation in which he does not have control, you can explain, "I give lots of choices, but this isn't something you have a choice about." Besides giving children a feeling of authority, this method lets them practice making decisions—an important life skill. It can also be used to guide behavior and highlight the consequences of negative choices. For example: "You can either finish cleaning your room now, or we can cancel the playdate you were supposed to have later today and clean up then." (Of course, you must be prepared to follow through on either choice.)

If you notice that your children are regularly uncooperative, chances are you're not giving them enough choices. Increase those opportunities and watch your child become much more accommodating.

QUESTIONS FOR REFLECTION

- How often do I tell my child what to do, when I could be giving her a choice?

- What specific choices do I remember giving my child today? Can I name at least ten?

TO DO THIS WEEK

- In each activity throughout the day (morning and evening routines, mealtimes, transitions, etc.) give your child at least two appropriate choices. If you proactively give options all day long throughout the week, it will become a habit.

WEEK  13

Discipline (Yourself)
Control: Be self-disciplined as a parent

People often confuse discipline with punishment, but in the context of parenting they're more like opposites. If you feel the need to dispense punishment, you probably lack discipline. Punishment is often arbitrary and in the long run, ineffective (see Week 9: *No More "Punishments"*). Discipline refers to a controlled pattern of behavior. Not for the *kids*—but for *you*. As a parent, you need to muster the discipline to be consistent in your responses to unacceptable behavior. If you can accomplish this, you will discipline your kids and have no need for punishment. Consider this: Researchers have found that uncertainty is the largest source of stress in babies and toddlers. When you aren't clear about what behavior is expected and which behaviors are not tolerated, your children are living in uncertainty every moment. If you tell your child to stop throwing the toy blocks, but then do nothing when he begins throwing them again, you have created confusion in your child's mind as to whether the behavior is allowed.

You must be disciplined about consistently taking action when your child displays inappropriate behavior or fails to respond when you tell him to do something. For example, if you tell your child to stop throwing the toy blocks and he throws a block again (even if he stopped throwing them for a while), you should immediately take away the blocks—and not give them back. Don't give in to whining, crying, or screaming. Don't give another warning, another chance, another *anything*. Your child now gets the clear message that if he throws blocks he will not be allowed to play with them. (He will have an opportunity to show that he can play with the blocks without throwing them tomorrow.) Following through *every time* with a consequence is crucial in creating an environment of stability, and it is an extremely effective method.

We often take out our anger on our children, when we actually might be angry with ourselves for not setting boundaries and letting behavior escalate. Taking immediate action keeps you from getting to the point where you lose your temper.

Again, the #1 thing you must do as a parent to eliminate struggles over discipline: *Be consistent!*

In the end, it's not about imposing "discipline" on our children. It's about *having* the self-discipline as parents to be clear about the boundaries we are setting and the lessons we are teaching. You don't *discipline* your children; you *teach* your children discipline by being clear in your own mind, and disciplined in your approach about what's acceptable and what's not. If you are consistent in providing consequences for behavior that is undesirable and positive feedback for behavior that is desired, you will eventually replace power struggles with family harmony.

QUESTIONS FOR REFLECTION

- Do I always provide predictable consequences for undesirable behavior, or do I find it difficult to be consistent?

- How often I often negotiate or give lots of warnings and/or second chances?

- In what situations do I take out my anger on my child?

TO DO THIS WEEK

- Be vigilant about not letting any undesirable behavior slip by without an appropriate consequence, keeping in mind strategies for providing logical consequences from Weeks 9 and 11.

- If your child doesn't respond to your first request, resist the urge to keep repeating the same instructions louder and louder. Take action (remove the child from the situation, take away what is being used inappropriately, or turn off whatever is distracting him from doing what you asked, etc.).

- Review the boundaries you established in Week 10 and make sure you don't ignore unacceptable behaviors at times, which is very confusing for your children. Dedicate yourself and stay consistent, especially with following through, as discussed in Week 7.

WEEK  14

Everything In Moderation

Self-Control: How to foster the fundamental concept of restraint

Put a four-year old child in a room with a marshmallow, and tell her that she will be given a second marshmallow as a reward if she avoids eating the first one for at least five minutes. Would you be surprised to know that whether the child resists the marshmallow can predict how well she does in school, how well she forms friendships, and how well she manages stress as an adult?

In the famous Stanford University "marshmallow study," scientists found this clear-cut correlation: on average, children who showed restraint as four-year olds were more successful academically and socially ten years later than those who were unable to exercise restraint. And a follow-up study showed that success continued into adulthood.

I probably don't need to tell you that babies are born without a speck of self-control. Infants have a natural inclination to grab whatever they want when they want it, but the parents' job is to help children slowly shed this notion of entitlement.

We should be working to raise children who are able to:

- Control their words and physical actions
- Exhibit patience and not always need immediate gratification
- Show and *feel* appreciation for what they have
- Cope with not getting everything that they want (without whining)
- Regulate their eating habits
- Withstand temptation
- Share and take turns
- Resist succumbing to the (negative) influences of others

So, how can you foster self-control in your own children?
1) First and foremost, you must *model controlled behavior yourself.* Children follow our actions more than our words.

- Keep your voice at an appropriate volume
- Choose your words carefully
- Show patience
- Conserve materials
- Model good habits (such as healthy eating)

2) Create real scenarios that will help your children develop skills of restraint. In small doses, provide opportunities and help them develop strategies for:

- Waiting
- Sharing
- Conserving
- Cooperating
- Giving feedback to each other

For example, bake with your child and take turns mixing. Have the person who is not mixing count to twenty (or mark time in another way, such as singing a song verse) before switching. Then tell your child that you are proud of the way she waited patiently.

Another example: teach your children to take modest portions when serving themselves food. Reassure them that they can always take more if they are still hungry after the first helping. Otherwise, they may take more than they may end up wanting— and wasting food that others could be eating.

3) Teach your children that they are not entitled to, and will not get, everything to which they take a fancy—regardless of whether you can afford it. Ironically, giving your child every material thing is not a form of love; it is a form of neglect.

4) Help your children appreciate what they have. Talk to them about the difference between "needing" and "wanting" using real-world examples. Involve them in charitable activities (see Week 33: *Just Do It*). Read and discuss books in which self-control or appreciation is the theme: *Did I Ever Tell You How Lucky You Are?*, *The Lorax*, and *Yertle the Turtle*, all by Dr. Seuss, are three of my favorites. An important note about developing self-control: expectations must be age-appropriate. The tips above are not meant for babies, who must have their needs met consistently in order to feel secure and loved. One doesn't spoil newborns by breastfeeding on demand, holding and cuddling them, and responding immediately to soothe and comfort them. And one can't expect a three-year old to sit quietly for half an hour with nothing to engage her.

But, while it is important to remember that newborns depend on us to have their needs met reliably, and that expectations for toddlers and older children must be suitable for their age, as with almost everything in this book, starting early is key. The part of the brain that is critical to inhibiting urges—the prefrontal cortex—is a work in progress and is not fully developed until early adulthood, but its development *begins* in infancy. Practicing self-control from a young age can help your children gain a level of restraint that will be critical for their schooling, happiness, and success in life. Remember that the next time you are on the verge of giving in to your child's spur-of-the-moment demand.

QUESTIONS FOR REFLECTION

For children younger than eighteen months:

• In what ways has my baby started to demonstrate the ability to self-soothe? Is she ever able to settle herself down or does she always need an adult to calm her?

For children older than eighteen months:

• Do I model restraint for my child? What are some ways I demonstrate strategies for self-control?

- What opportunities do I offer my child to develop self-control?

- Do I teach my child that she can't have everything she wants? Or, am I quick to give in to her material requests because I want to prove I love her?

- Does my child see me doing volunteer work? Do I involve her in age-appropriate charitable activities?

TO DO THIS WEEK

For children younger than 18 months:

- Always respond to your baby's needs. Babies need the security of knowing that they are safe and cared for at all times. This sets the stage for a relationship of trust between you and your child.

- Where appropriate, begin helping your child to self-soothe. Notice what successfully distracts her when she is upset (e.g., music, something interesting to look at, a "security blanket," etc.), and keep calm if she becomes just a little bit fussy, giving her a chance to settle herself.

For children older than 18 months:

- Give your child strategies to help her exercise restraint. For example, young children have difficulty refraining from interrupting others because they expect immediate attention and also worry that they will forget what they wanted to say if they have to wait. If your child wants to tell you something while you are talking to someone else and starts to interrupt, don't let her; instead, tell her you want to hear what she has to say as soon as a break occurs in your conversation, and then give her the strategy to hold her thought in her head until her turn comes to speak.

- Praise your child whenever she shows restraint (e.g., "I'm proud of the way you waited for mommy to finish her conversation with grandma before you asked for a glass of milk").

WEEK  15

Are Bribes OK?

Bribes: Don't get in the habit of using counterproductive inducements

B ribes are illegal in most of the world, and your home should be one of the places where they're "outlawed."

Sure, plenty of parents bribe their children to induce them to cooperate, but bribes create more problems than they solve. First, the obvious ones: Kids come to expect rewards for behaving well. Even worse, they learn that they can get big rewards by behaving badly, waiting for the promise of the big payoff, and then correcting their behavior.

A less obvious but equally important problem is that you want your child to do the right thing for the right reasons. Bribes will make your child believe that he does the right thing only when something's in it for him.

Consider cognitive dissonance—the surprising concept that people alter their beliefs based on their behavior. By bribing your child, you help him form a view of himself as a person who does the right thing only for big rewards. If you induce your child to do the right thing for better reasons without bribes or punishments, he comes to believe in the intrinsic worth of the right thing (see Week 24: *Belief Follows Behavior*).

Do not regularly bribe your child. Bribes will lead your child to behave the way you want *only* for a material reward. Instead of using bribes, let your children know that we all have responsibilities that we may not like, but that taking care of them leads to natural rewards: As soon as they do what they *need* to do, such as take their bath, they can do what they *want* to do, such as play a game with daddy. Word your encouragement carefully. Don't say "If you finish _____, mommy will get you [some material reward or food treat]", but rather, "Once you've finished _____, you'll be able to [do something fun that you like to do]." The difference is subtle, but the message you're communicating is vastly different.

On occasions you can allow children to earn stickers to mark progress and then give them a small reward when the chart is completed. Sticker charts can be an effective way of changing a child's ingrained behavior (especially a behavior that the child has no other inducement to change, such as giving up a pacifier or learning to use a toilet), or abolishing a bad habit (e.g., nail biting), or adopting a habit that will become reflexive (e.g., saying "thank you"). When the child completes the sticker chart, you can reward him with something like a special outing or a small toy that has been on his wish list.

Remember that using a sticker chart to hurdle a one-time hump is very different from rewarding your child for doing something you expect him to do regularly—such as cleaning his room (see my take on allowance in Week 37: *Allowance as a Teaching Tool*).

A ban on big rewards offered in advance doesn't preclude giving the biggest reward of all: strong expressions of love and approval. Kisses, hugs, and sweet words are the best reinforcements you can provide.

QUESTIONS FOR REFLECTION

- How do you motivate your children to do what you need them to do and behave the way you would like?

- Do you use bribes to try to persuade your children when they resist or induce them to act better in difficult situations?

TO DO THIS WEEK

- Pay attention to the way you induce your children to follow instructions. When you feel yourself on the verge of offering a bribe, stop and try a different tactic:

  First, calmly and succinctly let your child know why you need him to do what you've asked.

  Second, let your child know that whatever he wants to do next (e.g., play a game, have you read him a book, have dinner together with the rest of the family) will happen as soon as he does what you've asked. If appropriate, tell him what the negative consequences will be (e.g., he won't be able to go to his playdate, he will have to sit by himself to think about his misbehavior, he will need to allow extra time to get ready for bed tomorrow night since he took so much time comply with your request to brush his teeth). You don't need material rewards. You don't need punishments. Plenty of positive and negative consequences may be deployed (see Week 9: *No More "Punishments"*).

- Be very careful with the language you choose when there is an overlap between what might be considered a bribe ("If you eat your brocolli, you can have ice cream.") and what might be encouragement ("Green vegetables are important to help keep your body healthy. Once you've eaten the foods your body needs, if you're still hungry, it's fine to have ice cream.")

- If you have a one-time hurdle that you're trying to overcome with a child, create a sticker chart to keep track of a goal that you explain carefully to him (e.g., "Each time you let me know that you need to pee or poop and you do it in the potty instead of your diaper, we'll put a sticker on your chart. When you have six stickers, we'll have a special outing together, just you and me, to ride the carousel in the park.")

WEEK  16

What Really Matters

Priorities: Don't waste time on the small stuff

I see many families that, on the surface, have everything in order. But, what's really important? Consider these scenarios:

- The parents pack perfect lunchboxes every morning, but never sit down to breakfast with their children.

- The parents spend time making sure the home is spotless, but don't seem to mind that the children are disrespectful, constantly fighting with their siblings, calling each other names, and hitting each other.

- An eight-year old is scolded for not getting a perfect score on a spelling test, but his parents don't spend time reading to him.

- A mom asks what grade her daughter got on her test as soon as she walks in the door instead of inquiring about what interested her daughter in school that day.

You can see where I'm going with this, and maybe you see yourself in some of the examples above.

You have only so much energy, and parenting takes *tons* of it. If you devote attention and energy to things that don't matter as much, you automatically take time away from what *does* matter. So, you need to make a choice.

In the end, which is more important: That your family appears perfectly organized and together or your family creates an ambiance of respect, sensitivity, and self-control that leads to a happy family life and great kids?

I will admit, when my children were babies, their clothes didn't always match perfectly. With four children, if the color of someone's shirt clashed with his pants, it wasn't really cause for alarm. Some days, it was all I could do to make sure that everyone was wearing the essentials. But, the time and energy I would have invested to assure that my children were fashionable seemed better spent making sure that they treated each other well.

We all make dozens of decisions each day about how we spend our time. The key to making good decisions is to evaluate what truly makes a difference and what doesn't, not just on that day, but in the long run. If you concern yourself with a particular aspect of your children's life that is not going to contribute postively to your family's safety, health, or happiness in the long run, then you may want to consider if you're overlooking more important issues.

QUESTIONS FOR REFLECTION

- Do I have enough time to simply enjoy being with my children?

- Do I expend a lot of energy to get all the details right, but let bigger issues drop?

- Do I have the energy to provide clear boundaries and be consistent with my children?

TO DO THIS WEEK

- Notice the areas that command most of your time and efforts in family life and write them down. Also note what larger goals are missing. If you catch yourself spending energy on "small stuff" that doesn't really matter in the long run, try to change your priorities— first on your lists, and then in life.

WEEK  17

Interacting At All Ages

Relating: How you connect with your
children changes as they grow

We all know the importance of good parent-child communication, yet I often hear parents of teenagers say, "My child won't talk to me!" If you have a baby or young child, you may think you don't need to worry about this problem until your child hits adolescence, but I disagree. Patterns of communication between parents and children that begin in infancy set the tone for all later interactions.

The approach to good communication with your children should begin when they are born and change as they grow. From birth through early toddler years it's all about *talking*. Then, as your child begins to engage in activities, the importance shifts from talking to your child to *doing* things with your child.

In a nutshell: *Talk* more when they are babies and toddlers. *Do* more when they are older. This approach may seem counterintuitive, since babies are not capable of having conversations and older children are, but even infants respond to conversational patterns with their facial expressions, movements, and sounds (gurgling and babbling), and they begin to understand your words sooner than you think. Babies build social relationships based on verbal communication, and toddlers love to learn about the world around them through simple conversations.

From the minute we held our first child in our arms, my husband Seth and I spoke to him about what we were feeling, what we were doing, and what was happening around us, and I strongly urge other parents to follow suit. You may feel strange at first saying things like "Daddy went to pick up your grandma and grandpa, and he's bringing them back in a few minutes to meet you" while looking into the eyes of a day-old baby. Nonetheless, if you start speaking to your baby immediately in this way, conversation (albeit starting out one-sided) will quickly become a habit.

Scientists have found that a person's language ability is directly related to the number of neural synapses that develop mostly in the first six months and entirely in the first two years. Exposing a child to the sensory perception of language will stimulate the growth of neurons that facilitate language development. I am not suggesting that you discuss world politics or quantum physics with babies, but do comment on and explain what is happening in their immediate environment. Narrate for your baby what is going on in the world around him, put words to his feelings, and soothe and entertain him with singing.

Also, try repeating a set speech that is tied to visible actions they can regularly observe. For example, every time you dress your baby you can use the same language: "First Daddy pulls the shirt down over your head, and then he takes one arm and puts it in the sleeve, and then he takes your other arm and puts it in the other sleeve." When babies consistently hear the same words associated with specific actions, they begin to decode language.

In this way, you can develop a meaningful, mature, respectful practice of communication from the start. As your child transitions from baby to toddler, you will naturally continue the same respectful dialogue, but of course move on to more sophisticated subjects. For grade school students, seek out specific activities (see Week 21: *Attention, Please*) in which you interact and enjoy each other's company, because participating in pastimes with your children is a prerequisite to continued good communication.

QUESTIONS FOR REFLECTION

- Is my child in the "talking" phase of communication (approximately birth to age four), or the "doing" phase (age five and up)?

If he's under the age of four:

- Do I naturally provide an ongoing narrative for my baby/toddler? What kind of language do I use?

- How much of my baby's/toddler's day is he hearing people speaking to and about him? Do I talk to him while I change his diapers, ride in the car, do chores, run errands, etc.?

If he's four or older:

- Are my questions to my child (such as, "What did you do at school today?" or "How was your playdate with Justin?") met with shrugs or one-word answers? Do conversations feel like a bit of a struggle?

- What activities/interests/hobbies do I share on a regular basis (at least weekly) with my child?

TO DO THIS WEEK

If your child is younger than four:

- Take note of how often you speak to your child other than to give him directions. While young children certainly need some periods of silence, you should be communicating with them verbally for much of their waking time. Make a list of some opportunities for verbal interaction that you might be missing—while strolling him, waiting in line at the grocery store, making lunches, etc. This week, consistently interact verbally with your child during those times. It may feel a little strange at first if this is not your usual mode, but it will feel more natural over time.

- Pick one daily ritual (e.g., bath time, your morning routine) to narrate for you child and use the same language each day.

- For toddlers, talk about the new things they are seeing in the world around them as you go about your day. Answer their questions with interest and enthusiasm, and solicit their ideas with questions of your own (e.g., "Why do you think policemen wear uniforms? What's your favorite fruit?"). Play games that involve a back-and-forth dialogue (e.g., "I spy something big and yellow that has wheels. Do you see it? What do you spy?").

If your child is four or older:

- Make a list of things that currently engage your child's interest (e.g., music, baseball, the Civil War, spiders) and another list of the *types* of activities that he enjoys most (art projects, reading, being outdoors, building things).

- Come up with at least two activities that you can share on a regular basis. Brainstorm with your child. For example, you might decide to make a weekly outing to various beautiful natural settings where you sketch side-by-side and compile your drawings in a booklet. Or take a regular trip to the library to check out a mystery book. Maybe you could visit a different construction site each week. Perhaps you decide to build a model railroad together and reserve time each week for working on it. Or you might want to volunteer together at an animal shelter.

- Involve your child in the planning, set a regular day and time, and follow through.

WEEK  18

Parting Thoughts
Separation: Help your child feel confident

Whether it's on the first day of preschool, or on a planned night with a grandparent or babysitter, many children fall apart when their parents depart. While this anxiety is normal, some techniques can prevent separation from leading to a complete breakdown in discipline. First, as in all other matters of discipline, set expectations.

• Talk with your child in advance about the upcoming separation.

• Remind your child that she will experience anxiety about leaving you, reassure her that her feelings are natural, and describe what you expect in terms of behavior.

• Don't transmit to your child any of your own nervous or sad feelings about being apart—instead, approach the separation positively (relate what she'll enjoy about it) and let her know that you have confidence in her.

Second, try to engage your child with a substitute attachment. At home, have the babysitter begin reading her a favorite book, or have a sibling involve her in a game. At school, engage her in a classroom activity. This is a key step; if you try to leave without giving the child anything else to distract her, she will focus on the separation.

An important note here: do not sneak out on your children. Always let them know when you are leaving and assure them you will be returning. Sneaking out may procure one free pass, but will aggravate all future separations by making your child insecure.

Third, offer something for the child to look forward to after you leave. A project, a (healthy) snack you've prepared, a special job for her to do. I would often write notes to my kids to be read only after I left. Sometimes they were so eager to read the note (or, when they were very young, have it read to them) that they actually became impatient for me to leave. When kids are old enough, they can write a note (or draw a picture) for you to take with you and read when you're apart.

Finally, remember who's in charge. Sometimes nothing works, and, after all of your efforts, you find yourself trying to leave a crying, distraught child. In some circumstances you can't leave. (For example, many preschools will not allow parents to walk away while a child is crying; in that case, you will just need to keep trying the steps above.) If at all possible, don't put your child in charge by overly delaying your departure. It will only encourage further separation problems later. The child learns that the parent will stay if they put up a fuss.

By separating from your child assuredly, you will instill confidence in your child. Children almost always calm down very quickly after separation once they realize that the crying won't make the parent stay and that they have been left with things and people on which to focus.

QUESTIONS FOR REFLECTION

- Are separations from my child often difficult and drawn out? How do I try to ease separations?

- Do I wish that those separations would go more smoothly?

TO DO THIS WEEK

- Before the next separation, prepare your child (by talking, reading books that tell the story of a successful separation, etc.) and set expectations.

- At the time of separation, keep calm, engage your child with a person or activity, and give her something to look forward to later.

WEEK  19

Is Anybody Listening?

Communication: Show your children that you are paying attention

O n a recent day, I saw the following scenarios:

- A mother waiting in line at a store was listening to music on her iPod. Her son (about six years old) and daughter (about four years old) were hitting and shoving each other.

- A nanny was talking on her cell phone while she pushed a toddler in her stroller. The child was pointing to things they passed and trying out new words, but the nanny was unresponsive.

- A boy was sitting next to his father on the subway solving some interesting math problems out loud to amuse himself. Each time he asked his father a question, the father remained focused on his BlackBerry.

A national survey by The Henry J. Kaiser Family Foundation found that the amount of time children and teens spend engaged with electronic entertainment media (including computers, smartphones, TV and

MP3 players) has risen dramatically in the past several years. This probably comes as no surprise, but what the Kaiser survey *didn't* examine is how much time *parents* are connected to one electronic device or another, and how much of that time they're in the presence of their children.

Electronic devices are wonderful in many ways, but just as they distract drivers on the road, so do they distract parents and caregivers when they are with their kids. I am saddened every time I see a parent or caregiver ignoring a child (of any age, including babies) while they chat, text, or listen to music. These are missed opportunities for bonding, conversing, learning, laughing, reading, and sharing, and the child interprets the message: "I am not important."

Let me share with you a scene that I witnessed as I was riding on a city bus a few weeks ago; it warmed my heart: The mother of a little girl was chatting with her daughter about what they could see looking out the bus window.

"Oh look! There's a double-decker bus—your favorite! I wonder if the people riding on top outside are cold in this weather. What do you think?"

The girl gave a thoughtful answer and then exclaimed, "Look, that sign says t-o-y, toy!"

"That's right!" said her mother. "What would it spell if it said t-o-y-s?"

The girl proudly gave the answer and pointed out another discovery. The conversation continued in this way back and forth for about fifteen minutes. Then the mother offered her daughter a bag of Cheerios and said, "I'm going to take your doll out of your hands so you can hold your snack. Would you like me to hold her in my lap or put her in the backpack?" (She didn't ask whether she could take the doll—it wasn't an option—but she did give a choice about where to put it.) The girl responded that the lap would be better so that her doll could see out the window and the mother said, "Oh, that's right! I think this is your doll's first trip on the bus, so she will want to see everything. Let's look for more things to show her!" The conversation continued until they left the bus. The little girl had been cheerful the whole ride, clearly basking in her mother's mindfulness, and not feeling secondary to a cell phone or BlackBerry.

While multi-tasking might be productive for you and is sometimes necessary, it conveys the notion to your children that you don't fully care about them even though, of course, that isn't true. Being present in the moment gives your children the full stimulation that aids in their development. Also, the more focused attention you give your children, the more likely that you will receive it back in later years when your kids have many choices about their activities other than interacting with you. Your attention is one of the greatest gifts you can give your children—and yourself.

QUESTIONS FOR REFLECTION

- How often do I give my child my full attention?

- In what circumstances was I totally engaged with my child today and for how long?

- In what situations am I often distracted during time with my child? What keeps me from giving her my complete focus?

TO DO THIS WEEK

- Over the course of the next few days, take note of how often and for how long you use your phone, BlackBerry, iPod, laptop, etc. while you are in the company of your children, and whether you are really giving them your full attention when they need it.

- Determine which of those times you could have disengaged from your electronics. Many parents find it helpful to turn their devices off, if possible, so that they won't be tempted to "just check."

WEEK  20

Are You Over-Parenting?
Resilience: Don't shield your kids from lessons they need to learn

One of our desires as parents is to prepare our children to be self-reliant. That requires us to provide security, safety, and structure, yet not coddle our children. In short, we must not "over-parent."

Children are much more resilient than we often acknowledge. Although we naturally want to give our children everything they need, our job should not be to shield them from every little hardship or satisfy their every whim. Kids learn lessons from setbacks and disappointments and learn restraint from understanding that they can't have everything they want.

> "Although we naturally want to give our children everything they need , our job should not be to shield them from every little hardship or to satisfy their every whim."

We often do a better job parenting by helping our children figure out how to solve a problem themselves than by solving the problem for them.

Imagine you're leaving an activity with your child, and on your way home your child says, "I'm hungry." Do you stop and get your child something to eat right away, or do you tell him that you'll be home in ten minutes, and he can have a snack as soon as you arrive? If your child is having difficulty getting along with another child, do you intervene (through teachers or the other child's parents) or talk to your own child about ways he might handle the situation himself?

A corollary of not fixing everything for our children is to resist the temptation to solve problems that they can and will solve themselves. When a young child takes a little spill, perhaps at the playground, a parent is likely to rush over and exclaim, "Oh honey! Are you all right?" At that moment, the child, who often might just pick himself up and carry on with playtime before the parent rushes over, usually starts crying reacting to the parent's concern. When parents never give their children a chance to soothe themselves or overcome obstacles, children don't learn how to problem solve, a very necessary skill for succeeding in life. Of course, you should be ready and willing to help as necessary, but often it's wise to see what your child can bring to the process before jumping in to make everything "right."

Resist the urge to prevent your children from learning from their own mistakes or ever feeling disappointed. Children learn important lessons from dealing with difficulties and problems; don't jump in to fix everything for them. They will be better-prepared adults if you let them develop the coping mechanisms they need.

QUESTIONS FOR REFLECTION:

- How do I feel/react when my children suffer a slight hardship (e.g., your child complains about carrying his backpack, and you're two blocks from home)?

- When was the last time I let my child try to fix a problem himself?

- Do I have trouble letting my children be disappointed or feel the slightest bit uncomfortable?

TO DO THIS WEEK:

- Note the times you may be jumping in too quickly to make things easier or to solve problems for your children. Offer to talk with them and provide support, but don't immediately take over. See if they can either handle the disappointment or figure out how to solve a dilemma themselves.

- If your child comes to you with a problem, first listen and ask questions to clarify the nature of the problem.

- If your child is struggling to solve the problem on his own, help by giving options, but try to resist stepping in to fix things for your child unless the situation requires your intervention.

WEEK  21

Attention, Please
Individual Attention: Nurture each child

Every child deserves to have time when attention is focused entirely on him. If you have more than one child, make sure that you carve out time with each of them alone. You'll get more mileage out of a half hour alone with each child than several hours with all of your children together.

One-on-one time works best as a natural part of the daily schedule. For example, each of our children, as a baby and toddler, would sit in the infant seat or on the counter in the kitchen while my husband Seth prepared breakfast each morning. Seth would narrate every step of his breakfast-making routine ("I take four strawberries—one, two, three, four—and put them in the bowl."). Even though making breakfast may not seem exciting, our children loved this one-on-one time and came to know the routine and enjoyed pointing out the next item needed, etc.

Then there's bedtime. I am often asked whether to put kids who are close in age to bed at the same time for efficiency's sake. My answer is no—we always staggered our children's bedtimes in order to be able to put each to bed individually. Putting a child to bed is a moment of great potential closeness, and it should not be undermined by multitasking.

I also suggest regularly scheduled weekly activities with each of your children. For example, our son Tal is artistic and enjoys painting. I began taking a watercolor class with Tal when he was eleven, and he and I continued the once-a-week class for seven years.

Special planned activities or outings with each child are crucial in developing close relationships with each of your children. Let your child help plan the activity. One way in which I implemented these strategies was to sit down with the children every September and look through the season brochure for a theater that featured family programming. Each child picked out a show that he or she wanted to attend alone with me that year. The kids looked forward to carefully choosing the shows each year, and the outings were always momentous because of the planning and anticipation.

Immerse yourself in whatever activity you choose, and make sure you're not distracted by other demands. (If you are taking a hike with your child and you allow yourself to be interrupted by work-related cell phone calls, your child will come away thinking that he or she is less important to you than the rest of the world.)

Encourage relatives and close friends to plan activities with each child separately; our kids' individual trips with their grandparents were among their favorite childhood experiences.

This suggestion isn't just about having fun. Spending time alone with a child is one of the most important ways to demonstrate your respect for him or her as an individual.

QUESTIONS FOR REFLECTION

- What daily and weekly one-on-one experiences do I (and, if relevant, my parenting partner) already have in place with each of our children? Where are the gaps?

- When was the last time each child had a special outing alone with a parent or relative?

TO DO THIS WEEK

- Don't leave one-on-one time to chance. Plan a weekly activity with each child alone (e.g., gardening for a half hour, cooking dinner together every Thursday, practicing soccer in the park on Saturday afternoons). If necessary, make a chart or note times in your calendar.

- Plan a special outing for each parent with each child (e.g., an all-day hike, a trip to a special museum exhibit, a movie night).

WEEK  22

Put an End to Whining
Complaining: There is only one way to stop it

Whining is one of the most common irritants for parents, yet it is one of the easiest problems to solve. It's simple: children will continue to whine if, at least some of the time, they get what they want.

You should first convince yourself and then convey to your child that whining is an unacceptable behavior. Then you must *never* give in to your child when he is whining. If your response is not 100-percent consistent, your child will remember his whining "successes" and will intuitively think, "Hmm...sometimes when I whine, I get what I want. It's always worth trying." The key is to never let whining succeed.

For example, if a child whines, *"I'm hungry"* as a way to ask you for a snack, most parents would respond by offering something to eat, but that's a mistake. First, you should require a polite and respectful request. You could say calmly, "That's not how you ask for something to eat. Please try again." If your child doesn't comply, the consequence is that you don't respond with a snack. Let your child know, "As soon as you ask me politely for something to eat, I will respond to you."

Take another example: You're riding in the car and your child whines from the backseat, "I'm boooooored." Your reaction might be to immediately offer something to entertain your child, such as a game of "I Spy," or singing. Instead, you should first ask your child to express himself in a different tone of voice. You might say, "It sounds to me like you're whining. Is there something you want to tell or ask me?" Do not respond in any other way until your child says something like, "Can we do something to make this ride fun?" or (without whining) "I'd like something to do because I'm bored." If necessary, you can feed your child the words.

If your child asks for something in a polite way, you should acknowledge his favorable behavior (e.g., "I really liked the way you asked me!"). As I will discuss in detail in Week 24, cognitive dissonance has an extremely powerful effect. When a person continues to behave in a certain way (in the case of whining, it often happens because no one corrects it and it gets a result), the person will come to believe that the behavior is correct.

If you have zero tolerance for whining, your kids will quickly stop. You may find that prediction hard to believe, but it's really that simple. I promise, whining isn't heard in my home, and you don't need to hear it in yours!

QUESTIONS FOR REFLECTION

- Have I spelled out for my children that whining is not an appropriate way to make requests?

- When do I give in to my children's whining?

TO DO THIS WEEK

- Have a talk with your child about why whining is unacceptable. You might even use humor, demonstrating how it might sound if *you* whined all the time.

- Don't overlook any whining (even if you think it's "mild").

- Do not respond to whining by giving your child what he wants. Wait until after he expresses himself in an appropriate way.

WEEK  23

Who's In Charge?

Authority: You don't need to ask
your child's permission

I often hear parents use the phrase, "my child won't let me _____."
This miraculous reversal of authority ranges from the case of a three-year old whose parents say he won't *let them* leave the room when he goes to bed, to a seven-year-old whose parents say he won't permit them to buy a certain present for his friend's birthday party, to a thirteen-year old whose parents say their kid has to have the most popular (read: most expensive) brand of sneaker, to a high schooler who won't let his parents go to parent-teacher conferences.

I recently saw a couple with a three-year-old boy in an elevator. The husband hugged his wife, and the boy squealed, "No! Don't do that." The young mother shrugged off her husband's embrace, which prompted the husband to ask, "What's wrong?" The wife replied, "Johnny doesn't like when you do that." The husband, with a sheepish, almost guilty grin, relented. I felt like posing the question, "Who's in charge here?"

Parents *do not* need to get permission from their children for decisions that parents should be making themselves!

Have you heard statements like these from other parents or yourself?:

- "I always end up spending a fortune on sneakers because Gary insists on getting the brand that all his friends are wearing."

- "I have to buy the expensive ice cream. That's the only kind Julie will eat."

- "Joey insisted that his birthday be at the same arcade where his friend Eli had his."

In all of the examples above, the parent has abdicated the parental role, allowing a child's request to take priority over his or her own good judgment or desire. The parent is not only giving in to the child's demands, but is also missing a perfect opportunity to teach values.

Parents can—and should—maintain their family's priorities and ideals when challenged by more mundane, material concerns.

Which brings me to another trap into which many parents fall. Parents are too often swayed when their child says, "but Jenny's parents let her _____" (fill in your own example: watch R-rated movies, stay out until 1:00 a.m., have her own room, etc.). Other common examples are, "but all my friends do it" and "everyone has one." Do not be swayed by what other parents do. Make decisions based on your own family's principles and explain to your children how your decision reflects those ideals. Ultimately, your children will respect you for it and appreciate your consistent and meaningful standards.

Your child does, however, have a right to his privacy. Unless his safety or health is in jeopardy, you should, for example, ask for his permission to enter his room or reveal information that he may have told you in confidence.

Children are inclined to test parental authority, but being in charge is scary to them, and, in the long run, they are happier with knowing that you set boundaries and stick to them. You owe your children that comfort and security.

QUESTIONS FOR REFLECTION

- Am I in the habit of asking my child's permission?

- Do I sometimes hear myself say to others, "My child won't let me _____?"

- When have I given in against my better judgment when my child told me that other parents let their child do X or Y?

- Does my child give me orders? Do I respond to my child's demands?

TO DO THIS WEEK

- Listen carefully for any demands or commands that come from your child. Remind yourself (silently) and your children (out loud) that you do not take orders from them. You can certainly listen to and discuss their opinions and requests, but first be clear that they are not in charge of you, despite what may have occurred in the past.

- If you hear yourself say, "My kids won't let me," determine whether you have let your children make a decision for you that should not be theirs to make. Reevaluate the decision based on what you truly believe reflects your values and standards.

WEEK  24

Belief Follows Behavior

Reinforcement: An effective way to nudge children toward desired behavior

Belief follows behavior. This is the theory of cognitive dissonance: when a person's own actions contradict the person's beliefs, the brain (instead of changing the actions) tends to adjust those beliefs to explain the "dissonant" actions. The brain thus eliminates the dissonance by amending its opinions and beliefs.

You can use this knowledge in a number of important parenting techniques. Cognitive dissonance is one reason that parents should never say to a child, "You made a mess on the floor; you are a bad girl!" When the child makes a mess, which she knows she should not make, a dissonance is introduced—*I'm not supposed to, but I did it anyway*—and the child's brain asks itself, "Why did I do that?" If you provide the answer, i.e., because "you are a bad girl," then the child subconciously eliminates the dissonance by adjusting her view of herself, " I must have made that mess *because* I'm a bad girl." Don't accuse your kids of being "bad;" instead, work on changing the behavior by providing consequences (see Week 9: *No More "Punishments"*), and as the child begins to behave better, she will begin to believe that she is well-behaved, and in turn will tend to act that way.

Because belief tends to be based on actions, parents should encourage and praise children when they behave well to help instill the beliefs. Let's say you point out, "Carol, you have been very well-behaved and didn't interrupt while I was on the phone. You're very patient, and I'm proud of you." At that point, Carol thinks, "I was patient. Why was I so patient? I must be a well-behaved girl." You can have even more of an effect by adding, "I know how hard it is to be patient while I'm on the phone, but you didn't let your frustration make you misbehave." That remark increases the child's dissonance—"I not only behaved well, I did it even though it was really difficult. I'm *really* well-behaved."

When you tell your child, "Michelle, I was really happy when you asked for some milk with a 'please'; you are learning how to be polite," you plant the thought in Michelle's brain (whether that thought is conscious or not), "I *did* ask with a 'please' without being reminded. I must be polite." As Michelle starts to think of herself as being polite, she builds on that belief.

Cognitive dissonance is also the reason that you should be careful not to promise a child a big reward for good behavior. Big rewards—offered in advance—are counterproductive; instead of thinking she behaved well because she is a well-behaved child, a reward will make her think, "I just behaved well because I got a reward." (see Week 15: *Are Bribes OK?*).

Parents can employ role-playing with their children to extend the power of cognitive dissonance. For example, when you are having trouble with a child who is not interacting well with a friend, one possible solution is to act out the situation with you playing the part of the friend. You can guide your child's behavior on the desired path, and when she acts out the proper behavior (under your guidance), she will likely adopt the proper course of behavior as her own.

When children repeat desired behavior, they adjust their disposition so it's in line with their actions, unless they are given another explanation. The insight that belief follows behavior is a powerful concept; now you can use it as a strategy in your parenting toolbox.

QUESTIONS FOR REFLECTION

- Am I careful not to label my children when they misbehave?

- Do I reinforce desired behavior with explanations that will help my children view their actions as being consonant with their beliefs?

- Do I role-play with my children to "practice" positive behavior?

TO DO THIS WEEK

- Be cognizant of how you respond to any incidence of misbehavior, and take particular care to focus on changing the behavior and not labeling the child.

- Identify a particular behavior or behaviors that you want to encourage, and look for every chance to do so in a way that reinforces your child's beliefs about those actions. Keep track of each time you do this, and see if you can increase the number of positive reinforcements each day.

- Choose a specific issue your child is currently having with behavior, relationships, fear, or a source of stress. Role-play through the challenging situation with your child. Suggest possible responses to another person's behavior while you play the part of that person. For example, if your child gets physical with other children when she plays, pretend to be another child and take away her toy; then help her act out potential positive responses.

WEEK  25

Reasonable Responsibilities

Accountability: Contributing to the family should be the focus of age-appropriate chores

Children can begin simple chores at a very young age and should learn that pitching in is key to being part of a family; everybody is expected to help out. Allowance and chores should never be linked. If children are paid to do chores, money becomes their motivation, which is exactly what you want to avoid. (Contributing to the well-being of the family should be its own reward.) Moreover, children who are paid to do chores figure they can decide not to do their chores and not get paid. This type of policy puts the child in charge and sets up a power struggle.

> "If children are paid to do chores, money becomes their motivation, which is exactly what you want to avoid."

Requiring certain chores without payment accomplishes several goals: kids learn what it means to help out and not have everything done for them— an antidote to "entitlement." It fosters a sense of responsibility, and teaches children how to perform tasks that they will have to do on their own one day.

You can choose from many appropriate children's chores. Children can:

- Deposit their dirty laundry in the hamper
- Put toys away
- Keep their room neat
- Set and clear the table
- Make their beds
- Feed a pet
- Help make meals
- Sort laundry
- Help with gardening
- Rake leaves
- Sweep floors
- Put away groceries

Don't load on too many tasks, and avoid giving your children chores that you don't really care about—your children will know you're giving them busy work, and they'll resent it. Also, don't criticize your child's performance. Just use positive motivation to get the job done: "You did a great job putting those puzzles on the shelf. As soon as you put away the books we can play a game together."

If you need to impose consequences when they don't do the job, they should be logical and connected as much as possible to the chore. For example: "You haven't set the table, so we can't start dinner." A generic consequence allows the child to go onto the next enjoyable activity as soon as she completes the chore. An example: "You know the rule—we have to clean up from one activity before we begin the next. Now you have to put away your toys first before we can play your game."

Parents should be clear with their kids about what chores they expect them to do, and when and how often they should do them. If children are given a gentle reminder and parents follow through by having them do their chores before they play ("Do what you have to do so that you can do what you want to do" works well), the chores will become a basic part of their routine.

You can make a chore more fun if you sing, play music, or make a game of it (who can rake all the leaves in his section of the lawn the fastest?), but your child's biggest motivation to finish chores should be your show of appreciation and praise for a job well-done. "Thanks so much for putting away the groceries. You're a big help to me." Or, "You really did a great job cleaning your room this morning." Or, "I'm so proud that you remember to feed the fish every day without being reminded. You're taking very good care of them." When you consistently give your children positive feedback for their contributions, they will continue to contribute, and you will be on your way to raising responsible, cooperative family members.

QUESTIONS FOR REFLECTION

- In what ways do my children help out at home?

- What chores do I regularly expect them to do?

- Do I have trouble getting my children to pitch in?

- Do I end up doing things that I've asked my children to do, because it's easier to just do it myself?

TO DO THIS WEEK

- Assess each of your children's capabilities and determine several chores for which each can be responsible. Very young children can be assigned to "help" older children or parents.

- Download the "Chore Chart" from 52WeeksofParentingWisdom.com and fill it in. For chores that more than one child can do, alternate (e.g., one child does the chore one week and the other does it the next).

- Be consistent, and make sure that chores are done when they are scheduled and that your children don't engage in what they "want to do," before they do "what they need to do."

- Offer large doses of praise and appreciation for chores done well.

WEEK  26

No Fighting, No Biting!
Physical Force: Zero tolerance

I once saw a TV documentary about corporal punishment that featured a family with a hitting problem; daily life was a real "Thrilla in Manila." The parents themselves contributed to the physicality. "Johnny, don't hit your sister!" Wham! Johnny was slapped by Mom. "Suzy stop kicking your brother!" Wham! Suzy took one on the backside from Dad. What were the kids learning from all this violence? Was the punishment deterring the misbehavior? The punishment was modeling just the behavior the parents were trying to discourage.

Whether we are talking about siblings roughhousing or parents spanking, I am crystal clear on the subject of physicality among family members: there should be no physical contact between individuals other than affectionate exchanges. No exceptions.

What about kids wrestling with each other? Only if they are participating in an organized wrestling program. Nudging? No way. Shoving? Nope. Tickling? Not even.

"But children enjoy roughhousing," you may say. Well, they might enjoy it until someone gets hurt or begins to feel beaten down. We should be teaching our children that home is a safe place, and that violence of any kind is unacceptable.

It is not OK for grown-ups to push, slap, punch, or kick other grown-ups whenever they feel like it. Why should children have a different set of rules? If we allow children to release their physical energy (even in the guise of play) and take out their frustrations, anger, or any other emotions with physical acts, we are not doing our job of teaching them the restraint that they will need as they grow (review Week 14).

In order to execute a policy of no touching except to show affection, you must show zero tolerance. You must impose a consequence for every infraction (see Week 9: *No More "Punishments"*). It's not enough to say, "Don't kick your brother." At a minimum, you should require a sincerely delivered apology. (In my family, we always added a hug.) For anything but the most minor infraction, you must give an additional consequence; for instance, you can end whatever activity in which the violator was engaged. Whatever consequences you choose, they must include some negative result other than a reprimand. (No warning is required because your children will already know the policy.) As you know by now from reading this book, consistency is key.

If you doubt the wisdom of a no-physical-force policy, ask yourself, "What is the benefit of allowing physical force, ever?" A no-physical-force policy reaps huge rewards. I have children who never, ever hit each other, and who know they will never get hit by any of us. Without the inequality of power that results from unwanted physical contact, the family provides security and trust for every member.

QUESTIONS FOR REFLECTION

- Do my children nudge, hit, slap, kick, wrestle, or kick each other (or me)? If so, how do I react?

- Do I spank my children out of frustration or because I think it is an effective form of discipline?

TO DO THIS WEEK

- Commit to a peaceful home and make a decision not to allow any touching other than affectionate touching.

- Announce the policy to your children.

- Be alert to any infractions and act on them every single time. It may be tiring, but the hitting will stop if you are consistent about consequences. Refer back to Weeks 9 and 11 for a refresher on appropriate consequences.

WEEK  27

Inspire Confidence
Self-Assurance: Encourage adventurousness without bribing or nagging

Kids love repeating the same activities over and over, which is good; familiarity leads to comfort and security. Often kids don't want to try something different because it's new and feels scary. But children also have to learn to meet new challenges.

Your job is to entice your children to try new adventures without bribing (see Week 15: *Are Bribes OK?*) or nagging.

Here are some ways to achieve that:

• Offer your child a negotiable choice. When he suggests playing a game, say, "That's a great idea, and I want to go to the museum. I'll tell you what — you come to the museum with me now, and we'll play the game you suggest as soon as we return." (Behavioral economists have found that people tend to look past the first step in a two-step choice and focus only on the second. This is a wonderful insight for parents.)

• Offer the chance to take a first, small step. Instead of demanding that your child devote an entire afternoon to a museum, say, "Well, let's just go down to the museum and we'll see what's there." Your child might ask, "Do we have to go in?" You could respond, in an encouraging voice, "I think we'll find something you'll want to do there."

- Offer alternate choices that are unappealing. "OK, I suppose if you don't want to go, you could stay home and sweep the dining room." (Only offer this option if you are willing to follow through.)

- Once your child tries a new venture, make sure that you praise him for it. "I'm so proud that you took your first ice-skating lesson. Remember how you didn't want to do it? And, look at how well you did – you paid attention to the teacher and tried everything she showed you."

Each time you successfully introduce your child to a new activity, you make a deposit in his "confidence bank." Don't let your child's hesitancy hold him back; balance familiar activities with new endeavors, and he will gradually become more adventurous.

QUESTIONS FOR REFLECTION

- What are some recent situations in which my children tried new experiences?

- When my children resist trying an unfamiliar activity, do I let them off the hook too easily?

TO DO THIS WEEK

- Think of one new experience—a new game, a new place to visit, a new activity—that you could do with your child this week, and prepare him for it as much as possible ahead of time.

- Think about your child's approach to new experiences. Perhaps he doesn't want to go on a playdate unless you stay there the whole time. Ease him into it; tell him you are going to leave for thirty minutes to shop, but return and stay for the rest of the playdate.

WEEK  28

Manners Matter (No Matter How Young)

Politeness: The importance of "please" and "thank you"

Manners never go out of style. Not only do manners enable people to get along, they also play an important role in a child's development from a very early age (earlier than you'd think).

Showing common courtesy for others is an important practice because it is a sign of respect. Saying please and thank you, for example, tells others that you understand that they are not obligated to do your bidding. Having respect for others is one of the fundamental concepts we should all teach our children from a young age.

Some parents don't require their young children to say please and thank you because they believe that children can't understand the meaning of those words yet. But this theory misses the real point: Children will grow to understand the words' meaning by using them and will have already developed the habit of saying them. With your help, they also will come to appreciate why courtesy is important.

There are two general rules for raising polite kids. First, the earlier you start teaching common courtesy, the better. Children can learn to say please and thank you at a very young age ("bye-bye" is often one of a baby's first utterances). When saying these words becomes a habit, children get positive reactions to their polite behavior, which provides reinforcement. When they are respectful in small ways by showing common courtesy, they are more likely to develop that respect in other larger ways. Teach your children to say please and thank you as soon as they can form the words.

Second, be consistent. Children should be polite to their parents, siblings, relatives, and friends. If your child asks for something without saying please, wait for her to say the word before complying. Don't reward rude behavior.

Take every opportunity to point out examples of other people who use good manners. Also remember to give positive feedback when your child shows courteous behavior. For young children, acknowledge when they remember basic manners. For older children, recognize when they have shown courtesy in a particularly thoughtful way.

You are not asking too much of your children when you expect them to be polite. Rather, you are giving them a gift. It is extremely rewarding to raise children with these traits. At parent/teacher conferences, we were the most proud when our children's teachers told us appreciatively how polite and respectful our children were.

Winnie the Pooh, one of our family's favorite characters, says, "A little consideration, a little Thought for Others, makes all the difference." (Pooh may not be a genius, but his emotional intelligence is off the charts.) Teaching our children manners is an integral element in the quest to raise children who grow into respectful teenagers and eventually respectful adults.

QUESTIONS FOR REFLECTION

- Have I successfully taught my children to say please and thank you? Do they use please and thank you even in our own home among family members?

- Do I always model good manners for my children? For example, do I use please when I give them directions and thank them when they have performed any task I've requested?

TO DO THIS WEEK

- Pay attention to your children's manners. Make sure that they are using please and thank you whenever appropriate, even with family members. Start with this simple step, and then you can set other reasonable expectations: not interrupting others who are speaking (except in emergencies), saying a proper hello and good-bye when they meet people, and making eye contact when they speak with another person.

- Make sure you are consistently modeling good manners for your children.

- Proactively remind your children exactly what you expect of them before situations in which politeness might be an issue. (For example, when our children were young, we would remind them before going out to eat to thank the waiter or waitress when they were served. On the last day of summer camp we instructed them to thank each counselor for something specific, e.g. "Thanks for being my counselor and coming up with all those cool art projects!")

WEEK  29

Children Should Be Seen and Heard

Child-Adult Relationships: Include your children in conversations—starting at birth

Imagine having dinner with friends who spend the entire evening talking to each other about topics that they know don't interest you. You would most likely feel overlooked—possibly even hurt. Too often, children experience adult conversation that way. The adults chat in the front seat of the car, across the dinner table, and while they wait in line at the movies. The children say nothing—that is, until they become so bored that they begin to whine, interrupt, or argue with each other. Then the interaction usually turns into one of parents trying to 'manage' the children.

Of course, grown-ups need time to communicate with each other on adult topics, but these essential interactions should take place mainly when children aren't present or are otherwise engaged.

I was fortunate to grow up in a home where adults included children in most conversations. But in many homes, parents carry on conversations as if children aren't present, and they turn to the kids only to give them directions or to discipline.

If most of what you say to your children concerns practical matters—getting them to do chores, scheduling them, disciplining them—you may need to practice involving them in substantive conversations. You can start by bringing up something interesting that is happening in the world (the immediate world, for young children) and ask what they think about it. Kids are naturally curious, so when *they* ask a question, don't just give a perfunctory answer, initiate a larger dialogue.

Starting Early

Even children too young to talk should be included in conversations. When you are speaking to a friend or family member in the presence of your baby, pause intermittently to narrate what's happening. Your baby may not understand your words, but she will respond with facial expressions and gestures. Acknowledge her response—"Oh, I see."—and continue your conversation with the other adult, but return periodically to include your baby in the conversation.

When your baby begins to speak, you'll have to modify your discussions: take time to explain what you are talking about and start to incorporate questions she can answer.

As They Grow

As your children's sophistication increases, you can start to include them in conversations about all sorts of interesting topics. Ask, "What was the best part of your day?" Look for news about their areas of interest, whether it's sports, dinosaurs, trains, or music. Make sure every child is included and engaged in family discussions at his or her own level.

QUESTIONS FOR REFLECTION

- What percentage of my time in my children's company do I spend conversing with them? How much of that conversation is devoted to practical matters (directions, discipline, instructions, etc.)?

- Do I have long conversations with adults while I ignore my children?

- Do I sometimes talk to others as if my child isn't there?

TO DO THIS WEEK

- Make a list of possible conversation topics that your children might take interest in (current events, family news, a book or movie you've shared). Then brainstorm possible conversation starters for these topics.

- Think about ideal times for conversations (mealtime, while in the car, waiting in line at a store) and try some of your conversation starters. Then *listen* and build the conversation on their responses.

- Begin to include your children when you are speaking with other adults.

WEEK  30

Can't We Just All Get Along?

Siblings: A strategy for building on what they have in common

Relationships among siblings are the great proving ground for many of the aspirations discussed in earlier chapters, including setting clear and high expectations and helping your children develop restraint, respect, and sensitivity. More and more, social scientists are looking to a person's early relationships with siblings to divine the causes of all kinds of personality traits, both good and bad. Sisters and brothers live together, provide role models for each other, and reinforce each other's morals, beliefs, and manners. They provide the most frequent feedback and are the foils for testing social relationship skills.

A child whose older brother or sister drinks is twice as likely to have drinking problems compared to a child whose older siblings are teetotalers. A child with an older sibling who smokes is four times as likely to wind up doing the same as one whose siblings stay off tobacco, according to a Penn State study. The Penn State study also showed that, on average, children spend about a third of their free time with siblings. That chunk of time is more than they typically spend with anybody else, including parents and friends.

Other studies have shown that kids who can negotiate "peace treaties" well with their siblings can also resolve conflicts with friends and others outside their families.

In short, the way your children treat brothers and sisters will have implications far beyond your home. (If you have one child, you can apply the ideas in this chapter to relationships that your child has with relatives – such as cousins – or close friends.)

Here is a quick review of principles from previous chapters to apply to sibling relationships:

- Set clear expectations—There should be no hitting, shoving, or other violence (in fact, the only physical contact allowed should be the affectionate kind). Language used with siblings should be respectful at all times. (I am appalled by how some parents let siblings speak to each other.)
- Establish these expectations at a very young age.
- Be consistent.
- Explain the boundaries carefully, even to young kids. Well before a session during which siblings will be playing together, explain what your expectations are. For example, you can say, "In an hour, while I make dinner, you're going to play together. I want you to discuss any differences and try to resolve them by yourselves. If you can't, don't fight; come see me."
- Follow through to enforce the boundaries
- Use adverse consequences if necessary. For example, if your children begin to argue while they're playing together and don't settle the dispute when you ask them to, simply take whatever it is they're playing with away. The consequence for not being able to play a game together amicably is to not be able to play the game.
- Offer encouragement often when your kids play together well, show restraint, or display sensitivity toward a sibling.
- Give each child individual attention.

Beyond the application of these strategies, one of the best remedies for sibling rivalry is the cultivation of cooperation. Find ways to unite your children. One way is to identify activities, interests, and projects that your siblings can share. If you have more than two children, each configuration of sibling pairs should have something special to do together.

For example, our oldest son Shai, who was a math enthusiast, eagerly began teaching our youngest son Lev math games at a young age. Tal and

Shoshana formed a two-person music group, and each Saturday morning after breakfast they would spend time composing and singing songs while Tal played "drums" on a box; when they had new songs prepared, they would perform them for us.

The possibilities for shared endeavors are endless. They may last for years (or forever) or change as your children grow, but here are a few ideas:

- Play strategy board games
- Read to each other
- Create artwork together (which can sometimes be for specific occasions, such as drawing a picture for Grandma for her birthday)
- Build and play with a model train set
- Do science projects together
- Share a recreational sport
- Take a class together (two of our kids earned their SCUBA diving certifications together)
- Write and put on "shows" together, e.g., create a puppet show to perform
- Build and organize a collection, e.g., coins, stickers or baseball cards

When children have a shared goal and/or interest they will *want* to spend time together. In addition, they will see that there are many ways they can help each other and that doing so makes life much more pleasant.

Even though they're grown up, our children still talk to each other every day from college and visit each other often. Establishing bonds between your children over shared interests will create positive and respectful relationships, as well as wonderful mutual memories when they grow older.

QUESTIONS FOR REFLECTION

- Is our home a "safe" environment where every child feels respected and is treated well by siblings? Or are my kids often fighting, either verbally or physically?

- How do my children support each other?

- Do my children enjoy each other's company?

- What are our rules and consequences for how our children treat each other? Do we let some infractions slide to avoid having to referee?

- What shared projects or interests are my children working on, and do they pursue them regularly?

TO DO THIS WEEK:

- If you don't already have a set of house rules about how your children treat each other, write them down on a large poster and have a family meeting to go over them with your kids (see 52WeeksofParentingWisdom.com for a sample "Family Rules for Respect" as a starting point).

- Focus your attention on "zero tolerance" for any unkind words or actions between your children. For example, if one of your children makes a snide comment about a sibling at the dinner table, say firmly, "It's not OK to speak about your brother that way. We can't have unkind words in this family, so sit quietly on the couch in the living room for five minutes to think about how you can speak in a nicer way. When you've sat quietly for five minutes, I will let you know that you can come back to the table and join us as soon as you apologize to your brother." (The apology must include stating what the apology is for.)

- Think about activities and hobbies that your children might enjoy doing together. If you have more than two children, keep in mind the various pairs of siblings (a chart might be helpful). This week, schedule a time for each pair to engage in their shared interests (or sign them up for the class, etc.) and then build those activities into your regular schedule (on a daily, weekly, or other basis).

- Make another chart of things that each child can do for her siblings, again including all possible pairs. Take into account each child's capabilities and talents, e.g., Aaron will help test Ben on his weekly spelling list before Ben's quiz on Friday; Mia will entertain baby Linda in the bathtub while Mommy washes Linda's hair. Make sure that each of these interactions happens at least once this week.

WEEK  31

Activities: Too Many or Too Few?

Schedules: Find the right balance in your child's week

We all want our children to participate in activities that enhance their development. Yet kids need ample time to just relax, play with siblings and friends, learn how to pursue activities independently, and, as they grow older complete chores at home. Over-scheduled children are often tired and irritable, and, as a form of rebellion, they stop applying themselves to their activities. Children who are under-scheduled may be bored and could miss out on opportunities to find their passions. How should parents decide on extracurricular plans for their children? No magic formula can determine a child's optimum schedule, but you can come up with the best combination of outside activities for each child by looking at several factors.

Your Child's Personality

Does your child enjoy unstructured time, or does he become bored and restless when he doesn't have a plan? Some children feel stressed by always having to be somewhere at a particular time and relish the opportunity to have a free afternoon. Others like a very structured day and thrive when they have scheduled activities. Some kids love to be challenged; others are stressed when the demands are high.

Time Commitment and Intensity Required for Each Activity

Look at the mix of your child's activities in terms of the level of commitment and performance expectations. For example, my daughter loved ballet classes at the "Mommy and Me" and "Pre-Ballet" levels. But once the classes became more serious (including a requirement that she take a minimum number of hours per week), she became less enthusiastic. She was willing to spend many hours each week on other activities she enjoyed, but not on ballet. We were able to find a more appropriate recreational dance program for her, and she was much happier.

Make sure your child isn't overloaded with intense extracurriculars and be sure that the activities requiring a large time commitment are the ones he enjoys most.

Your Child's Interests

Does your child like group activities? Playing sports? Or does he prefer to spend hours drawing or reading? Know what your child is passionate about and schedule accordingly; make sure his schedule reflects his interests, not yours. For example, our second son loved to build all kinds of things when he was young—model kits, free-form structures, furniture for his sister's dolls. These projects required long spurts of unscheduled time, so we scaled back on all but a few organized activities.

Other Responsibilities

Take into account any demands on your child's time that are nonnegotiable. Does he have religious school, a long commute to and from school, or a lot of homework? Figure these responsibilities into your equation as structured time.

Keep in mind that your children don't have to stick with the first activities they try. Offer various activities when they are young and see what they enjoy most. Possibilities include programs or lessons in art, sports (team and individual), acting, chess, language, photography, computers, and music. Check out offerings at museums, community centers, libraries, and cultural institutions.

Reevaluate your child's activities at the start of each school year or semester. When your child wants to take on a new activity, or if you decide that he has too many, ask him the following question about each activity in his schedule: "Is this something you look forward to and would really miss if you didn't do it?" In this way, you can rank each program and decide what might be cut. Pay close attention to your child's demeanor when you have this discussion; the choices offered and made during his young years may ultimately determine his passions.

QUESTIONS FOR REFLECTION

- What percentage of my child's non-school time is spent in structured activities and what percentage is free time?

- Does my child have enough time to do what is required (schoolwork, religious school, etc.) and be able to just relax?

- Does my child have at least one extracurricular activity that will expose him to new pursuits?

- Does my child have one or two scheduled activities he really enjoys?

- Is my child over-tired, stressed, or not getting enough sleep due to over-programming?

TO DO THIS WEEK

- Using the "Activities" worksheet from 52WeeksofParentingWisdom. com, write out your child's current weekly schedule.

- Examine how this schedule corresponds with your child's interests and personality, as well as the level of commitment required for each activity, to see where adjustments might be necessary.

- Let your child help determine which activity (or activities) might be dropped, added, or modified depending on what you learn from the above exercise.

WEEK  32

Humor Helps

Comic Relief: Effectively using
laughter to teach

My youngest son can do a mean French accent, including a spot-on impersonation of Inspector Clouseau from *The Pink Panther*. It's such a surefire way to crack up our family that we often ask him to perform it for us. And, sometimes, he and I have entire conversations Inspector Clouseau-style, until we can't continue because we are laughing so hard.

Parenting is serious business, and it can be overwhelming, so we sometimes forget that laughter and fun go a long way to make family life pleasant. Not only does humor create a joyous atmosphere, but it is a wonderful tool for teaching.

Way back in Week 8: *Great Expectations*, you worked on preparing your child for unfamiliar situations by walking her through possible scenarios. Humor can play a big part in this strategy.

You can ask your children how they would respond in various situations, and try to throw in lots of humorous possibilities. You might say: "What should you do if you are leaving the birthday party, and the host is not handing out gift bags? Do you not mention the gift bag and say, 'Thank you for having me to your birthday party. It was fun,' or do you say [exaggerating here] 'Hey! Where's my gift bag? I gave you a gift, now where's mine? I'm not leaving until I get something!' or do you throw yourself on the ground and cry uncontrollably?"—pretending to cry can add to the amusement. Ridiculous choices like these always made my kids crack up when they were young, but I made sure they repeated the correct answer out loud—no matter how obvious—and they got the message.

Another way to teach with humor is through stories. Kids love humor in stories, especially the kind when one or more of the characters are so clueless that even the kids can get the joke. Want to give your kids a lesson in sharing? Tell a story with a stuffed goose and a stuffed panda bear duking it out over a toy truck and have the animals ultimately realize that they can take turns with the truck. A silly twist (such as the goose and the panda bear discover that the toy truck is too small for either of them to use) will delight your kids.

My daughter and I still break into hysterics each time we recall the story I once told with a few Barbie dolls and one Ken doll when she was five years old. It started when she wanted to use her entire collection of dolls in the story. Ken proposed to several different Barbies that day and when they all found out, they were none to happy about it. Ken showed no remorse. At the end of the story, Ken accidently fell off a cliff (the edge of the couch) and got his comeuppance. Perhaps the lesson was that we needed more Ken dolls (or fewer Barbies), but I like to think that my daughter also came to understand the importance of making sure she is treated well by others and that those who are devious and unkind do not deserve our friendship.

Learning while laughing—what could be better?

QUESTIONS FOR REFLECTION

- Is the sound of laughter regularly heard in our home?

- Do I employ humor to teach lessons?

TO DO THIS WEEK

- Let yourself be silly.

- Prepare your child for an experience by using humor to run through possible scenarios.

- Pick an issue you're working on with your child and tell a funny story to help teach the relevant lesson.

WEEK  33

Just Do It

Community Service: Start kids volunteering at a young age to curb entitlement

The phrase, "Your child is so thoughtful" is music to every parent's ears. What if your child isn't so thoughtful, and no one is singing his praises? What if your child is whiny, bossy, and demanding? Your child might have a bad case of entitlement. As parents, we try to attend to all of our children's needs and desires in order to keep them comfortable and happy. We also provide luxuries, such as a good education, toys, TVs, computers, and vacations. Sometimes they simply take these luxuries for granted. Children display a sense of entitlement by making demands and whining about insignificant things. Eradicate the problem now, because children with a sense of entitlement usually grow up to be adults with a sense of entitlement.

Start by teaching your children how fortunate they are. An effective way to do this is to expose them to the problems of the less fortunate. Seeing and helping others in need increases children's sensitivity to others and appreciation for all they have. Set an example yourself. Give to charities, do community service work, and share your efforts with your children. Talk to them in an age-appropriate way about what you do and why you do it. You can start this dialogue even when your children are toddlers. By the time they are four, you can start to involve them in community service projects, which you can do together.

Here are just a few ideas:

- Make sandwiches for donation to food banks
- Visit the elderly
- Serve meals at a soup kitchen
- Collect and deliver clothing and toys to organizations such as the Salvation Army
- Sign up for planting and cleanup efforts in neglected parks
- Write letters or make cards for those who are sick or serving in the armed forces

Include your children at a young age in charitable activities related to the holidays (e.g., a holiday toy drive, "Operation Santa Claus"). These pursuits will remind them of the needs of others at times they associate with abundance in the form of holiday meals and presents.

Community service projects help make the world a better place, contributing to the environment (recycling campaigns, litter cleanups, tree planting), health (walk-a-thons for research), politics (volunteering for a candidate) and more. For younger children, neighborhood-based efforts are especially appropriate because contributing to their community allows them to see the results of their efforts. In addition, regularly discuss important social issues with your children and solicit their ideas for things they can do to make the world a better place. They can help you research the websites that list the many volunteer opportunities for kids in your area. Finally, when your children whine, "It's not fair" about some petty wrong that has befallen them, talk to them (don't lecture) about the *real* injustices of the world. When they say they need the latest American Girl doll, video game, or basketball shoes, enlighten them about the difference between *wanting* and *needing*. Loving and providing for your children doesn't mean giving them everything that they want—it means teaching them to appreciate what they have. Involving them regularly in community service will help them become caring kids.

QUESTIONS FOR REFLECTION

- Does my child seem to have a sense of entitlement?

- Is my child aware of problems in our community and the larger world?

- To what extent is our family (grown-ups and children) involved in volunteer activities?

TO DO THIS WEEK

- Research volunteer opportunities for kids in your community. Brainstorm with your child about what you can do together to make the world a better place. Choose at least one volunteer project in which to participate on a regular basis and make a list of other one-time projects to engage in for the coming year.

WEEK  34

Mealtimes Together
Family Meals: Explore all options

A study by The National Center on Addiction and Substance Abuse found that teens who have fewer than three dinners per week with their familes are twice as likely to have tried cigarettes, 50 percent more likely to have tried alcohol, and twice as likely to have tried marijuana, as compared to children who shared five or more dinners weekly with their families. Studies have also found that kids eat healthier foods when they eat with their families.

Some parents argue that other quality time they spend with their children compensates for the lack of dinners together, but according to researchers, family connectedness that is developed through other bonding opportunities does not replace having meals together. A study found that even among families with high levels of family connectedness, when children had seven or more meals each week together with their families, they were significantly less likely to be troubled by alcohol, cigarette, or drug use than were children whose families had similar connectedness, but had one or no meals together each week.

Why are family meals so important? A host of reasons includes the fact that they are one of the few activities during which parents and children meet face-to-face. Family meals present occasions to practice respect and self-control because, at a meal, everyone has to learn to listen to others and wait his or her turn. Regular family meals also add structure, security, and a feeling of control to family life. You can engage in cooperative conversation (e.g., the day's schedule, upcoming events, news) so that it is both an enjoyable experience and bonding opportunity.

Obviously, this subject is a sore one for many families with conflicting schedules that feel sitting down to dinner together is unrealistic. I suggest that you take a less rigid view of the concept. Expand the idea to include meals aside from dinner. My family is often not home at the same time for weeknight dinners; instead, we eat breakfast together every morning, and it has become one of my family's most important traditions.

Determine how you can best maximize the number of meals you have together, even if it isn't every single day—perhaps weekend lunch or brunches and Friday night dinners might work for your family—and then make those meals together part of your regular family routine. Be creative. In China, many children eat dinner right after school, whether or not their parents are home; later, they sit and have tea or fruit while their parents eat dinner.

The advantage of eating breakfast together is that no one is otherwise engaged. In fact, if everyone gets up with the earliest riser, then by definition, everyone is available. Also, at breakfast you can talk about the day's upcoming activities so that schedules can be coordinated. Waking up early enough to make a real breakfast (though a bowl of cereal with fruit or a fruitshake is our normal meal) takes time and commitment, but the benefits outweigh the costs. Of course, if dinner works for your family, that can certainly be the "mandatory" family meal.

You may not be able to have every meal together, but whatever alternative you choose, you should not overlook the intangible benefits of family meals, and you should try to schedule as many as possible on a regular schedule. If you establish a positive routine, I guarantee that you and your children won't see it as a burden; you will cherish it as a family tradition.

QUESTIONS FOR REFLECTION

- How often does our family sit down at our table for a meal together?

- Do I require everyone to be present at certain meals?

TO DO THIS WEEK

- Analyze your schedule (with the help of your children if they are old enough) and determine realistic times for regular meals together. Scheduling family breakfasts, lunches, and dinners may involve some reshuffling and reorganizing, but it's worth it.

- Decide for which meals presence will be mandatory.

- Go over rules with your children , including the minimum length of time everyone will sit at the table and asking to be excused from the table.

WEEK  35

Passion Pending

Activities: Allow your children to discover what they really love to do

O ne of the greatest gifts you can give your children is to help them find what they love to do. When your children are young, expose them to a wide range of topics and activities and see what sticks. Try not to have preconceived notions about their likes and dislikes (especially notions based on your own preferences). Read books on various subjects, go to all sorts of events, and sample different activities. If you have trouble persuading your child to try new pursuits, re-visit Week 27: *Inspire Confidence*. Pay attention to what generates enthusiasm and nurture those interests. Follow your child's lead; once you've begun to uncover each child's particular passions and talents, participate actively in those interests.

Our daughter Shoshana took an early interest in marine biology, so we trekked to aquariums, devoted some of our beach time to exploration, and set up a fish tank in her room. My husband would look for newspaper and magazine articles to share with her. We encouraged and helped her when she launched a project to convince local restaurants to stop serving endangered fish.

I am not suggesting that every activity be focused on your child's interests. On the contrary, your child should learn to participate in the favorite activities of other family members. Nonetheless, some of your efforts should be geared to embracing what your child loves.

Ultimately, you want to help your children discover what art education expert Sir Ken Robinson, in his book "The Element," defines as "the place where their passions and talents intersect."

QUESTIONS FOR REFLECTION

- What varied experiences have I offered my children to help them explore what interests them?

- Do I follow my children's lead when their curiosity is sparked?

TO DO THIS WEEK

- If you are still trying to find out what floats your child's boat, provide several new experiences. Check out a book from the library about a new topic, visit a new point of interest, or try a fresh activity.

- If you already know what your child's current passion is, look for a new way to participate in it together.

WEEK  36

The Power of Stories

Processing: Use narrative to help children process their day

Children are constantly trying to make sense of their experiences and the world around them. You can help that process by telling them stories.

Wait, you may think, *I don't have a good enough imagination to tell stories.* Luckily, you don't need to think of any new material.

In fact, during the first few years, you can simply tell your child the story of his day: "Once upon a time, there was a little boy named ____. One day he woke up very early and he was happy when his mommy came into his room. She pointed out his bedroom window and said that it was raining. He was sad because he wanted to go to the park and play in the sandbox, but he didn't let his disappointment ruin his day. His mommy helped him dress for breakfast and told him that they would be visiting grandma today. She put on his favorite red sweater with the picture of the dinosaur on the front and made him yummy scrambled eggs. And..." Children *love* to hear the details of their day recounted in this fashion, and it helps them integrate events with their emotions.

As children grow older, employ stories to work out issues or challenges or to impart simple lessons. Use puppets, stuffed animals, dolls, super heros, dinosaurs—any "actors" will do. Center the story plot around whatever conflict is occurring in your child's life. For example, if cooperating with playmates is a current challenge, tell a story where one of the little animals always wants to have his way, and present various consequences.

With young children, you can tell the whole story yourself, but from the time they're four or five they may want to participate. Take turns, and, when they run out of ideas about what should happen next, take over for a bit and then let them jump back in. Eventually, your children will be able to initiate and tell stories themselves. Follow their lead, and throw a twist into the story occasionally to help it along.

We live in a world where content is available to children at the touch of a remote control, a computer key, or a video game control, but creating one's own stories is an important tool for developing oral language skills, fostering imagination and processing life lessons. Incorporate story-telling into your playtime, and soon your children will rank story time as one of their favorite activities.

QUESTIONS FOR REFLECTION

- When might I find opportunities to incorporate storytelling into my child's routine?

- What topics might be good jumping off points for stories to engage my child?

TO DO THIS WEEK

- Brainstorm potential story ideas based on your child's daily routine, events that are happening in her life, a lesson you want to teach, or a problem that needs to be solved.

- Try your hand at telling a story several times this week, either by narrating with words alone or by acting a story out with puppets, toy characters, dolls, or stuffed animals.

- For a story that deals with a conflict, create several false solutions before arriving at a satisfactory ending.

- If your child is old enough, let her participate in the story-telling.

WEEK  37

Allowance as a Teaching Tool
Allowance: Teach money and math skills; don't bribe

Many believe that allowance should be earned, but allowance should never be tied to chores or good behavior (see Week 25: *Reasonable Responsibilities*). Allowance can be a wonderful tool to teach children about money and give them the opportunity to practice math in a real world application. But it is *terrible* as a reward system; it sets up an ongoing struggle and instills the wrong beliefs in your child (i.e., "I am helping out because I'm getting paid," instead of "I'm helping out because I'm a good kid, and because contributing as a member of my family is important").

To avoid disputes about money, I suggest that you cover all necessities—food, clothing, shelter, education, instruction, good-quality educational toys and games—as well as presents for birthdays and holidays. As you might expect from my thoughts about restraint, I have a relatively narrow definition of "necessity," and I suggest that you adopt one, too (review Week 14: *Everything In Moderation* for my tips on teaching children the difference between "needing" and "wanting"). If your children want any additional "luxuries," let them pay for them out of their allowances or put them on their "gift lists" (see Week 39: *The Gift List*).

At age four or five (when they are beginning to acquire math skills), children can start receiving a small weekly allowance (50¢ or $1), along with encouragement not to spend it right away. They will quickly see how money accumulates if they choose not to make impulse purchases. (You can keep their money in a safe place or just keep track of their "account" on paper, giving them the money when they choose to spend it.) You can add any small cash gifts they receive from relatives or friends for their birthdays or holidays to their account. You should deposit gifts of large checks (say, more than $25) in a special bank account for your child and turn it over to her when she is old enough to manage it responsibly. (My husband and I picked age thirteen, but you can choose another age.)

With my children, although their weekly allowances were meager, they got 5-percent interest every month on the money in their accounts. For example, a child who had $10 in her account would earn 50¢ interest at the end of the month. (You can determine for your own children the amount you give each week, the interest rate, and the time period during which the family account will operate. Do your math carefully, however, because the compounding of interest at 5 percent per month is hard on the "bank.")

This arrangement taught our children restraint by rewarding (at a high interest rate) saving over spending. Each of our kids would see desirable things and wonder out loud, "Should I buy it, or wait for more interest?"

The family bank account system also provides an opportunity to teach math to your kids; even if they don't learn percentages as four-year-olds, the accounting will at least help them understand the usefulness of numbers (and the power of compound interest). When we ended the system for each child at age thirteen and deposited funds from their allowance accounts into their real bank accounts, they saw the paltry interest that banks offered, but the lessons of savings had stuck with them.

The bottom line is that you can give children a modest allowance—just enough for small items a child might fancy—and instill math abilities and self-control at the same time.

QUESTIONS FOR REFLECTION

- How effective is our allowance system as a tool to foster our family's values, as opposed to a system that rewards them for doing things they should be doing as a matter of course?

- Do I use allowance to teach my children about math and money?

- Does my allowance system encourage entitlement and excessive consumption or does it encourage self-control?

- What do I want to provide for my children and what do I want them to buy with their allowance? How much money do I need to give them for allowance so that if they save, in a reasonable amount of time, they will be able to afford something they want?

TO DO THIS WEEK

- If you already have an allowance plan in place, you may decide to modify it in keeping with your family's values. If you feel it's appropriate after you reflect on the questions, develop a revised plan and present it to your children.

- If you don't have an allowance system in place, consider devising one based on sound principles and implement a system as soon as possible.

WEEK  38

Avoiding the Picky Predicament
Eating: Cultivating healthy habits

I know parents who insist that their child will eat only one food, so they serve him that food every day. Not only are those parents failing to provide proper nutrition, they are failng to educate their children about an important topic. Perhaps even more important, those parents are shirking a crucial area of parental responsibility.

Explain the importance of a balanced diet so that your child understands why you're serving some foods and not others, and why dessert cannot substitute for the main course. Even toddlers can understand that some foods are good for you and others (even though they are tasty) are not. (Never try to induce a child to finish a meal by promising dessert; the healthy foods on the table should be consumed because they're healthy.)

Of course you can't force a child to eat, but you can control what you buy and serve, as well as what is not eaten. A hungry child will eventually find something to eat if you offer him a variety of healthy foods.

Do not become a short order cook—that just encourages pickiness. Make a family meal and (barring allergies) expect everyone to eat it. If a child

> "Do not become a short order cook – that just encourages pickiness!"

refuses to eat what you offer, allow him to take something healthy (a yogurt, carrots, a piece of fruit) from the kitchen so that he won't go hungry, but don't prepare a separate meal for him and don't serve him dessert.

At the same time, respect your child's wishes about food. I'm not contradicting myself. What I mean is, when you're packing your child's lunch or snack, offer several (healthy) alternatives. Take him shopping and allow him to pick the vegetables or the main course for a meal.

As you offer explanations and kids start to understand them, they become curious about and more conscious of health and a healthy diet. This way, when they're on their own, they don't necessarily view the time as an opportunity to break free of the shackles of their parents' diet. Instead, they will want continue to treat their bodies well. (Cooking together provides a great opportunity to share some of these lessons.)

Why do I suggest the two-pronged approach—simultaneously taking charge and respecting your child's wishes? First, I know from experience with four children that it works. Second, it is consistent with all of the principles you've learned so far: high expectations (Week 3); respect (Week 6); priorities (Week 16); limits with love (Week 10); self-control (Week 14); no bribes (Week 15); interacting at all ages (Week 17); individual attention (Week 21); who's in charge (Week 23); encouraging adventurousness (Week 27); minding manners (Week 28); and mealtimes together (week 34). Indeed, studies show that childhood obesity is correlated with *both* a permissive parenting style (giving children too much freedom) and an authoritarian parenting style (too little freedom, which causes kids to rebel). Take the middle ground and be authoritative about the classes of foods your child should eat, but let your child choose among acceptable alternatives.

QUESTIONS FOR REFLECTION

- Does our family often have struggles around mealtime and healthy eating?

- Is one or more of my children a picky eater?

TO DO THIS WEEK

- Speak to your children about healthy foods and about a change in strategy. Offer them a choice about which healthy foods they want for the week. Take them shopping to purchase the selections. If necessary, do a little research yourself so that you can explain why certain foods are healthier than others

- Stop catering to your child's finicky behaviors. Serve the same meal to the entire family.

- Try preparing unfamiliar foods in several different ways, and give your child a choice of healthy options. (The question shouldn't be whether he'll eat vegetables, but *how* he'd like to eat them.)

- If a child won't eat adequate portions of the foods you serve and is still hungry, offer a healthy substitute.

- Do not use dessert as a bribe.

WEEK  39

The Gift List

Impulse Control: What to do
when your children want stuff

How do you respond when your children ask you to buy them the latest toy, video game, or footwear? Perhaps you give in to your children's entreaties more than you would like. Or maybe you've grown tired of hearing yourself say "no."

Providing your children with everything they want is a bad idea (even if money isn't an issue); you'll miss the important chance to teach children restraint and that "wanting" is not the same as "needing." On the other hand, arguing about each request when it is made, or simply saying "no" reflexively isn't the answer. Fortunately, I have another approach.

My method of imposing restraint, without unnecessary strife, is to create a gift list for each of the kids. When one of them sees something he or she wants, I tell him or her that I will put it on a list of potential gifts for the next birthday, holiday, or other special occasion (whichever comes next). When we return home, we write the item on that child's gift list. When they were young, the kids took great pleasure in reviewing their gift lists regularly, perhaps almost as much pleasure as they would have enjoyed from having the gifts themselves. In any event, the list satisfied their immediate craving. Then, when birthdays and holidays rolled around, they would know what to request when relatives asked for gift suggestions.

The beauty of the gift list is that it teaches self-control and helps avoid wasteful impulse purchases. I often found that well before the gift-giving occasion rolled around (and sometimes even by the next time we looked at the list to add a suggestion), items on the list were already out of favor, and we would cross them off. This process was also instructive for the kids—they saw on their own how many of their wants were mere whims that changed even before they could acquire the item.

My one exception to the gift list was when we went on vacation. On these excursions, I allowed each child to pick one souvenir during the course of the trip. Again, this eliminated any struggles and also encouraged each child to be thoughtful about his or her alotted purchase.

Employing the gift list option when your children make requests is an incredibly easy and effective solution to a nagging problem. Once you implement this strategy, you'll never again have to deal with that terrible tug-of-war when your children see something that they (think) want.

QUESTIONS FOR REFLECTION

- When my children ask me to buy them things do I argue (or feel like arguing)?
- Do I usually give in to their requests so they won't be disappointed, or do I find myself responding with an automatic "no?"
- Does every "no" turn into a negotiation?

TO DO THIS WEEK

- Next time your child covets something on TV, in a store, or at a friend's house, establish and explain the gift list. (Note: You can find a handy "gift list" feature on my ParentSmart app). Make sure your child sees you add the item to the list. Let her review the list as often as she wants. When a birthday or holiday comes around, reevaluate the list, then use it as a guide for gift giving (by you and others).

WEEK 40

Culture Connections I
Music: Incorporate music into daily life

Music is a great way to incorporate several of the principles covered in earlier chapters; learning a musical instrument is consistent with setting high expectations (Week 8); interacting at all ages (Week 17); encouraging adventurousness (Week 27); balancing activities (Week 31); and finding a pending passion (Week 35). Moreover, if you want a happy, joyous home, music can contribute to that.

Once, when our son Shai was preschool age, we were at a restaurant where a violinist was performing. Seeing a young child in the audience, the musician broke into several children's songs, and Shai immediately identified each one. The violinist upped the ante and played a classical piece; his jaw dropped when Shai matter-of-factly said, "Oh, that's Peter's Theme from [Prokofiev's] 'Peter and the Wolf.'" Even by the time he was two, he loved to listen to music and could often "Name That Tune."

Because I trained in piano at a conservatory, music has always been a big part of my children's lives. Starting as soon as they could sit upright in my lap, I played the piano and sang with the kids daily. But you don't need to be a musician to expose your kids to music. My husband has no musical talent, but he regularly listened to music with the kids. Their favorites were Raffi, Laurie Berkner, and Pete Seeger.

In addition to listening to music and singing with our kids, we always kept a box of musical instruments—drums, cymbals, maracas, xylophone—out in the open in the playroom for the kids to play when the spirit moved them.

We required each of our kids to study a musical instrument of their choice. They all chose piano, which was not surprising given my piano playing. None of our children have chosen music as a career, but all of them say that their lives are enhanced by their appreciation of music.

I often hear adults say, "I wish I studied an instrument" or "I wish I hadn't given up lessons," but I can't ever remember hearing anyone express regret that they studied an instrument. We chose to require music lessons for our children until age thirteen—three of our four children opted to continue through high school.

If you don't require your children to study an instrument for a minimum number of years, there are many other ways to make music part of your child's education. Share music you like with your kids, and as they become teenagers, let them share music they like with you. Take an interest in their choices; they are more likely to respect your preferences if you show respect for theirs.

QUESTIONS FOR REFLECTION

- Is music a part of our family's daily life?

- What is my relationship to music, and how do I want to share it with my children?

TO DO THIS WEEK

- Think about how you want to incorporate music into your children's lives (e.g., playing in the home more often, taking music classes, attending concerts). Start or make plans to start whatever activity you choose this week.

- Share at least one musical activity (even if it's just singing in the car or lulling your children to sleep with a lullaby) each day.

WEEK  41

Untraditional Traditions

Holidays: Establish unique customs
that will keep your family close

When they talk about plans for upcoming holidays, people often mention spending time with family and friends, travel, meals, shopping for and giving gifts, and parties. These holiday traditions are wonderful, but what *special* traditions does your family have?

Traditions help kids understand their world, and according to researchers, foster feelings of security and reduce anxiety about the future. When you incorporate your family's own interests and styles into traditions, those benefits will accrue even more. The customs you put into place will have much more meaning and make the connection to family even stronger for your children.

Find a way to create your own traditions. For example, if your son is a train buff, make it a tradition to visit a holiday train display. Perhaps you can enjoy a yearly sporting event, holiday show, or circus together, or a favorite movie no one ever tires of gathering together to watch on New Year's Day. Maybe it's a physical acitvity, such as a Fourth of July hike. A friend of mine who likes to bake spends several days making hundreds of holiday cookies with her daughter each Christmas, and then they deliver them to friends. The tradition can be one that reminds your children of their heritage. Or it can revolve around volunteering; our family, starting with my grandparents, has served breakfast together for men in a drug rehab program every Christmas morning for more than twenty-five years. Our children became involved as soon as they were old enough to contribute even in just a small way, such as helping to set the tables.

Keep in mind that family traditions alone do not make a strong family. A family may have a ritual of taking a camping trip every Memorial Day weekend. That sounds good, but if the family doesn't take the members' various interests into account, the tradition won't have the desired bonding effect and will more likely breed unpleasant relationships, boredom, or chaos. So make sure to plan your traditions in conjunction with the other principles outlined in this book.

Generic traditions are good. But rituals that are particular to your family and your children's interests can be even more special. Those experiences will be what your kids talk about during the year, anticipate with excitement as each holiday approaches, and look back upon fondly as they grow up.

QUESTIONS FOR REFLECTION

- What were my favorite family traditions as a child?

- Are there ways we celebrate that are unique to our family?

- What will our children remember about our holiday celebrations when they are older?

TO DO THIS WEEK

- Make a list of any activities that you've done with your children during recent holidays or special occasions other than the usual holiday fare (e.g., going to watch fireworks on the Fourth of July is fine, but it doesn't count for our purposes here), and note any that you might potentially instill as annual traditions.

- Think about whether your family had any one-of-a-kind customs when you were growing up that you remember fondly and that you might like to reinstitute with your children.

- Think ahead to the next holidays and come up with plans for "trademark" activities, such as those you may have tried that are worth making part of your annual routine, or some that you remember that you'd like to institute anew. Note them in your calendar and talk with your kids about them to increase anticipation.

WEEK  42

Bond Over Books

Reading: Establish routines with your kids at all ages

My husband and I started reading books with our children when all they could do was sit in their baby seats and stare. As the months passed, they came to know those books and loved to hear one of their favorites—or a new one—read to them over and over.

Once our children graduated from basic picture books to simple stories (at around age two), we would often choose books that had a moral or ethical message, and we would discuss that message with our kids while we read the book. We looked for stories that exemplified our favorite themes: restraint, respect, and sensitivity. The books enabled us to show our kids that we were not the only ones interested in these values. (You can find a list of some of the books and series that I recommend for teaching these principles at 52WeeksofParentingWisdom.com.) Likewise, we were careful to steer clear of stories that seemed to condone the opposite of those qualities—namely entitlement, insolence, and insensitivity. Surprisingly, many books on the market provide models for unattractive behavior, and you should be careful to steer clear of these.

Books are also a perfect way to work through an issue your child may be having, whether it's a behavioral problem, a fear, or a specific situation she is encountering. You can effectively use books as a jumping off point for discussing emotional topics and problem-solving (sometimes called biblio-therapy). Likewise, the right book can help prepare your child for an upcoming event or milestone, such as toilet training, attending school for the first time, going on a trip, or a new baby in the family. When children read about how others negotiate life's challenges, it provides them with encouragement.

Of course, make sure the books you choose are age-appropriate. I often see parents reading books that are far too complex, including picture books with too much clutter on a page for a baby to take in, or a story book with text too dense for a three-year-old who loses interest. When you choose chapter books, a general rule of thumb is to look for books where the main character is approximately the same age as your child.

You should read with your children with enthusiasm and heart; do not treat it as a rote chore. Reading provides an opportunity for physical closeness with a baby on your lap or an older child snuggled up next to you. To engage with your child, stop and ask questions, point out themes and morals, and ask for input about how characters might be feeling. Some of the most wonderful inter-actions I have had with my children have been during our reading together.

> "To engage with your child, stop to ask questions, point out themes and morals, ask questions about how characters might be feeling, elaborate, explain, or discuss."

Reading with your children costs nothing, but it's priceless. Read with your children every day. It's as simple as that.

Starting Early

Many people don't think about reading to babies, but parents should engage infants interactively to foster language development. Show them the pictures, point to different objects on the page, and say the words. In a short time, you'll be able to ask your baby, "Where is the car?" and she'll be able to point to the picture of the car. Bring books to life by acting out what's hap-pening on the page with your baby (e.g., clap her hands together) and enhance with sounds (e.g., animal noises and sound effects, such as "whoosh"). Babies can even begin to learn when to turn pages of their favorite board books.

By about the age of eighteen months or two years, your children will know some parts of their favorite books (particularly simple rhyming books) by heart, and you can begin teaching them to read. My husband or I would sit with one of our kids on our lap and read a book while we pointed to the words. When we'd reach the end of a sentence, we'd stop before the last word and just point. Our kids usually knew the word, and soon they could read it. As is the case with many skills, kids can learn by doing much sooner than they can master the abstract concepts. Teaching kids to read early can give them a real confidence boost (see Week 27) as well, because belief follows behavior (see Week 24). Get them to read early; the experience promotes bonding with you and will attach them to reading for life.

As They Grow

Just because your child might not need a bedtime story anymore, doesn't mean that you shouldn't continue to read together. Our children still read with us into their teen years, alternating with us as the reader out loud. If you keep the tradition going—classics, popular series, non-fiction, or even newspaper or magazine articles—this bonding experience doesn't have to end.

Now one of our great joys is to watch our older kids read to Lev, our youngest. Shai started him on the Harry Potter series, and Shoshana loves serving him up such classics as "Tom Sawyer;" she even skypes with him from college so they can read outloud together. If that's not a testament to the bonding power of sharing books, I don't know what is.

QUESTIONS FOR REFLECTION

- Do I read with my children every day?

- Do I choose books that impart values and behaviors that I want to instill?

- On what topics might I employ books to help my children through life's challenges?

TO DO THIS WEEK

- Look at your schedule and see how you might work more regular reading time into your children's lives. Write down your plan. With your child's help, pick a book to read together.

- Analyze closely the kind of reading materials you're sharing with your children. Note down where your selections might be lacking and take a trip to the library.

- Make a list of topics you might like to explore with each child (e.g., a story about starting school for the first time) and then ask your librarian for recommendations.

WEEK  43

Family Trips

Travel: Keep everyone engaged
and happy on vacation

F amily trips (movie spoofs aside) are a core activity that can combine
fun, learning, and family togetherness. Sometimes, however, vacations can be frustrating because the various family members' desires
are at odds. I have an overall vacation strategy that addresses this problem
and has been very successful throughout our twenty-two years of taking
family trips together.

Whenever my family starts thinking about a trip, my husband and I
consult the kids and offer them choices. We involve them in the planning,
and when we decide where to go, we confer with them about what to do
when we arrive. This policy shows that we respect them (see Week 6: *Those
Who Give Respect Get Respect*). We don't simply drag them along; we treat
them as full participants. Sure, you must sacrifice some of your dominion
to give choices to your kids (see Week 12: *Choices Choices...*, while keeping
in mind Week 23: *Who's In Charge*), but the benefit to the development of
the family is completely worth the sacrifice.

Planning a trip that will engage each member of the family isn't com-
plicated. First, set down any necessary parameters for your vacation, such

as duration and how far you are willing to travel. ("This year we are going to take a five-day vacation and we are going to visit places by driving—no plane flights." or "This year we are going to Canada for ten days.") Next, gather ideas from your children about what types of destinations might interest them within that framework. You may hear, "I want to go somewhere where we can play on the beach," or "I'd really like to go to the Baseball Hall of Fame." If a child's first request cannot be incorporated into the trip, offer possible substitutes. Finally, gather everyone in the family for a meeting and discuss the options and the planning.

For example, in 2005, my husband and I decided we would like to travel with the kids to the West Coast of the United States. We wanted to visit and stay with one of my friends for a few days, and we knew that other constraints would shape our thirteen days of travel. We had many interests to juggle, including marine biology, golfing, national parks, and historic sites, and we managed to plan a trip with whale watching, sports, Sequioa National Park, and several musuems.

When you plan a trip like that, each child enjoys the activity specifically chosen for him, and, in most cases, is enthusiastic about his siblings' interests as well. If one child has an alternative activity that he really wants to do or if a scheduled activity is not age-appropriate for one or more of the children, we simply split up for a few hours.

During a trip, we always share in the execution of the plan. Each day, we put one child in charge of choosing optional activities, one child supervises navigation, and one child selects places for meals. Obviously, you must set the parameters, but then the child in charge solicits the opinions of all the siblings, learns about the possibilities from you, and makes a decision. For example, the navigator might look at the map, study routes with you, and ask who wants to drive by the ocean and who wants to drive by the inland parks; after everyone voices an opinion, the navigator chooses. The day's activity leader might use the same procedure to choose among a movie, a fair, or a fireworks show. You can actually create a chart at the outset of each trip so that each child knows which day he is assigned which task (very young children can be assigned to "assist").

This technique of involving everyone in the planning and execution of the trip can be adapted and used no matter the type of vacation you take. If a child is too young to participate in the decision-making, the siblings must learn to represent that child's needs as part of their planning. The crucial element is that everyone has a voice; if you accomplish that, an enjoyable experience is almost sure to follow.

QUESTIONS FOR REFLECTION

- How have my children been engaged in planning our previous trips?

- During our vacations, have we taken each child's particular interests into consideration?

TO DO THIS WEEK

- Begin to think about your next family trip. Start a discussion with your children, perhaps over dinner, about what they would like to do on vacation. What interests would they like to have accommodated if possible? Strategize the ways in which each family member might be satisfied. Incorporate these ideas into your plans, and let the kids participate as much as possible.

- If you have an upcoming trip, print out and use the "Trip Planner" from the 52WeeksofParentingWisdom.com website to give your child/children assignments for each day.

WEEK  44

The Best Birthdays

Celebrations: Send the right message with your child's party

Our family has vivid memories of the birthday parties we threw for our children when they were little. Why? Because each party was unique. We threw a "polar bear party" (in the middle of June), a "superhero spectacular," a "teddy bear picnic," a "subway adventure," and a "fairy tea party," just to name a few.

If you feel overwhelmed by the idea of planning your child's birthday party, welcome to the club. Birthday celebrations are a source of stress for many parents, but your child's party can actually be a joyful experience if you focus on what's important.

Birthday parties are an opportunity to:

• Celebrate your child's individuality.

• Show your child how much she means to you and how much you care about her interests.

• Convey your family's values.

- Teach your child to create wonderful things with effort, resourcefulness, and inspiration.

- Give your child happy memories.

Step one: Pick a theme that resonates for your child. If you don't already know what she is absolutely crazy about, find out. You can turn any theme into a party—from a favorite color, animal, or story, to a favorite activity. The only criterion is that it's something your child loves. Our themes have included the beach, Winnie the Pooh, sports, robotics, trains, dinosaurs, game shows, and Willy Wonka's Chocolate Factory.

Step two: Brainstorm kid-friendly, age-appropriate activities that stem from the theme (without carefully planned activities to keep children engaged, the party will descend into chaos). You can capitalize on a theme in myriad ways, including cooperative games, art projects, cooking, various kinds of hunts (e.g., treasure hunt, scavenger hunt), obstacle courses, and memory games. You can take it one step further and write an imaginary story line for the entire party and link the activities with the story as it unfolds.

For example, for my youngest son's train party on his fourth birthday, we created a train by decorating and painting large cardboard boxes. Sammy the Steam Engine sat inside our front door with a sad face (taped on). We explained to all the party guests that Sammy had derailed and lost his cargo, and he needed their help. In each room of our house was a game set up relating to each of the train cars (cattle car, circus car, etc.)—for example, in one room the children had to hunt for spilled coal (hidden pieces of crumpled black construction paper) and return it to the coal car. After they completed all the activities, the children went to the dining room to hear a story ("The Little Engine That Could") and eat birthday cake (shaped like a train). In the end, they were delighted to find Stanley with all his cars filled and a big smile (taped) on his face.

Creating a tailored party for your child definitely takes thought and preparation, but the process itself can actually be a lot of fun and a wonderful collaborative experience for the family. When we planned parties, my husband and I let the birthday boy/girl choose the theme, but then we planned the details in secret, often with help from our other children.

If you can't (or don't want to) hold a party for umpteen children in your home, perhaps friends or relatives will be willing to lend you their place, or you can rent a room at a party space or community center. I encourage parents to be the key figures in planning and running the party (even if you hire someone to lead a special activity). Your child will know that you put the time and effort into creating a magical party geared to her passion, and that will make all the difference.

QUESTIONS FOR REFLECTION

- Do I feel overwhelmed by the idea of planning my children's parties?

- Do I feel pressured to create an extravaganza that might not represent our family's values or keep to an appropriate budget?

- What is my child interested in/obsessed with right now that might inspire a party?

TO DO THIS WEEK

- Start brainstorming for your next birthday party. Solicit themes from the birthday child and then list possible activities centered on that theme. Use my "Birthday Party Planner" (available at 52 Weeksof-ParentingWisdom.com) for inspiration and organization.

WEEK  45

Culture Connections II
Creativity: Incorporate the arts into daily life

During one winter vacation, my children decided to make something with the small shells they had collected on the beach. I whipped out some white glue, and we created shell sculptures—an impromptu art project. Back in New York, we decided the sculptures would make lovely decorations for our goldfish tank and were sure that our fish loved the home improvement. Several hours later, as I walked past the tank, I did a double take when I saw the fish struggling in gooey, white water. Apparently, the glue we had used was water-soluble. In a panic, we scrambled to prepare new water and remove the fish from the tank as quickly as we could, saving them just in time.

So, I don't recommend displaying your child's artwork in the fish tank, but when I walk into a family's home and see no evidence of artwork or creative projects done by children, I wonder if an opportunity is being missed. Creativity is a natural quality in all children, but as parents, we have a responsibility to nurture it.

Many parents unknowingly transfer their own feelings of insecurity about their creative capacity to their children.

> "Many of us unknowingly transfer our own feelings of insecurity about our creative capacity to our children."

They justify the lack of creative endeavors in which their children participate by saying, "Johnny isn't interested in art." Or, "I can't even get Susie to color with crayons. She is bored by art."

Your children might actually be gravitating away from art because of the sense that they are not good at it. That's why it's important that you help them avoid preconceived notions about how art "should" be. Parents should offer enough options for a creative outlet so that kids can find what medium they enjoy—whether it's crafts, painting, woodworking, sculpting, photography, or building structures.

I think that every house should have an art supply area with paper, markers, glue, scissors, stickers, paints, colored sand, colored tissue paper, felt, Play-Doh, clay and lots of odds and ends for collages. When your child picks up shells at the beach and says, "Maybe we could make something using these," you instantly have potential art materials.

Avoid art kits that involve nothing more than assembling precut pieces—they don't do enough to foster your child's creativity. On the other hand, an art kit that encourages imagination is much better. For example, one that contains instructions and supplies to make something like pompom animals may allow the child to decide how the creature he creates will look, especially if you encourage him to imagine designs other than the suggestions shown on the box.

When a project is completed, you'll want to celebrate it, but be sure to admire the process ("I like the way you mixed the colors," or, "You were creative in designing the roof"), *not* the product ("That almost looks like a real house.").

What do you do with all the projects that pile up? Label and save all of them, at least for a while. Every few months, go through all your child's artwork with him, choosing two or three items for display and other pieces for permanent storage in an art portoflio (which can be bought in an office supply store or simply made from large sheets of cardboard). Rotate pieces between storage and display.

The point is not that your children will become fine artists (though they may). It's about finding an outlet for their creativity and giving them permission to use it. When you nurture your children's creative spirit, you give them a gift of confidence that will serve them well as they begin to enter a grown-up world where practicality is often the top priority.

QUESTIONS FOR REFLECTION

- Do I nurture my children's creativity?

- Do I praise my children's art by focusing on the process, not the product?

- Do I show respect for my children's artwork by displaying and saving some of it?

TO DO THIS WEEK

- If you don't have one already, establish an art supply area in your home.

- Engage in at least two creative projects with your children this week.

- Figure out the best places in your home to display artwork, both the pieces that can be hung and those that need a shelf.

- Label each piece with a name and date immediately upon completion. Store everything temporarily, and go through the cache with your child every three months or so to select works for display and permanent storage.

WEEK  46

Cooking Lessons
Cooking: Food preparation offers many lessons for kids

Kids love to cook (I use the term loosely—any type of food preparation counts), and it is a wonderful activity that provides unlimited opportunities to apply many of the parenting methods covered in prior weeks.

My husband and I involved our children in meal preparation from the time they were babies. They sat in an infant seat and watched us while we narrated the process in detail and with gusto (sometimes we even sang). Once they could sit up, they could hold things (e.g. measuring spoons), and eventually they could begin to perform tasks with a little help, such as mixing and pouring. During the preschool years, we baked almost daily with full participation from the kids, from measuring ingredients to cracking eggs.

Every weekend morning from the time our eldest son could sit in a baby seat until our youngest was about six (a span of sixteen years!), my husband would have one of the kids watch and/or help make breakfast pancakes. He would patiently explain to them step-by-step the process of making pancakes, from counting spoonfuls to explaining fractions of cups, to the science of why the expanding air bubbles in beaten egg whites keep the pancakes fluffy. Cooking is a fun sharing activity, an opportunity to reinforce values, and a vehicle for conveying skills and knowledge.

My husband would also make another point in his pancake-cooking sessions. The recipe for pancakes that he developed makes tasty pancakes from whole oats, raw almond nuts, tofu, banana, and eggs, plus a couple of spoonfuls of honey and whole wheat flour. So each session would also serve as a lesson in healthy eating. No activity will pique kids' interest in nutrition more than actually spooning the ingredients into a bowl (see Week 24: *Belief Follows Behavior*). Your kids will actually come to enjoy a food not just for its taste, but for what it can do for their growth and health (see Week 38: *Avoiding the Picky Predicament*).

Cooking can also play a part in family traditons and cultural customs. Every year, on the Jewish holiday of Purim, our family bakes batches of hamentaschen—triangular cookies associated with the holiday—from a special recipe passed down through my husband's family. We then share the fruits of our labor by distributing bags of the cookies to friends and families.

During our children's preschool and elementary school years, we also baked with their friends on a regular basis. Our kids' friends loved having playdates at our house because they almost always baked something, and they got to take home some of the cookies or brownies.

Cooking together is really the perfect adult–child activity; it can be shared at all ages and provides lessons in language, math, science, fine motor skills, nutrition, patience, taking turns, sharing, and family traditions. I don't know any kid who doesn't enjoy baking, and if you start when the children are young, it may become an activity that you can share as they mature. My kids all still enjoy delving into a recipe together (or inventing a new concoction of their own), and they have fond memories of our times in the kitchen when they were little.

QUESTIONS FOR REFLECTION

- How often (if ever) do I involve my children in kitchen activities?

- Do I use cooking as a teaching opportunity?

- What meal(s) or dish(es) during the week could I make with each of my children?

TO DO THIS WEEK

- Set aside a time this week to share a cooking project with your child—even a very young child (you can find some recipes to start with at 52WeeksofParentingWisdom.com). Make it fun and relaxed (don't worry about the mess) and take advantage of the teaching opportunities as they arise.

WEEK  47

Is TV Bad?

Television: Know what your kids are watching and watch with them

People often ask me if I let my kids watch TV—and if so, how much. I respect families who choose not to allow television watching (my family didn't have a TV when I was growing up), but I don't think television is inherently bad. It can, in fact, provide opportunities for learning, fun, and family bonding. If you decide to have a television in your home, you must establish policies from the start and stick to those policies. Most important, you should: monitor *what* your children watch, set clear boundaries about *how much* they watch (I suggest setting a boundary such as no more than one hour a day), and *talk* to them about the shows they're watching.

My kids watched *Sesame Street* when they were little, but we did not require them to stick to educational programming. They also watched sitcoms (such as *Full House*), sports, and game shows. As they grew older, they liked to watch drama series, news, and reality shows. But my husband and I insisted on one clear boundary until they were thirteen—they had to ask us before they could watch.

If you require your children to ask permission to watch TV, you will always know what and how much they are watching. It's best to set this boundary early on, before kids might be resistant; but if you didn't do that, don't be discouraged; you can institute it at any age (see Week 23: *Who's In Charge?*).

Select certain TV shows to watch together; it offers a great opportunity for all sorts of interesting and instructive discussions. If they see behavior that is inappropriate, you can explain to them that it is inappropriate and talk about why. Even commercials provide a learning opportunity, or at least a chance for shared amusement. These conversations will enable you to convert a supposedly passive activity into a little sharing, a little learning, and a little fun—what every family activity should be.

What other policies should you set? I recommend the following:

• No TV for babies.

• No TV while doing homework or studying.

• No TV during meals (given the importance of conversation at mealtimes).

• Take away TV privileges only if losing those privileges is a *logical* consequence of some undesirable behavior (e.g., a homework assignment was forgotten and not completed because your child was too engrossed in a show).

• No TV in the bedroom.

Keep in mind that you can't monitor what or how much children watch if you put TVs in their rooms. This may seem obvious, but about 70 percent of young children have TVs in their rooms, even as early as in third grade, and parents of those children significantly underestimate how much TV they are watching. (One study found that having a bedroom TV increased the average children's viewing time by nine hours a week.) A TV in the bedroom also correlates with increased obesity, sleep disorders, and academic struggles. One reason that a kid's bedroom TV watching is far worse than other TV watching is that it tends to be a solitary activity, while family TV watching can be much more.

You should be as disciplined about TV-watching rules as any other aspect of your child's life. Make sure that the boundaries are clear to your children and implement proper follow-through so the rules stick. Let expectations about what your children are allowed to watch—and when—evolve as they grow older.

If you have clear TV-viewing rules, are selective about what your children watch, and often watch with them, television can be an opportunity for connecting and learning.

QUESTIONS FOR REFLECTION

- Do we have clear policies about TV watching in our home?

- Have we made these policies clear to the kids?

- Do we follow through with those policies?

TO DO THIS WEEK

- Take stock of what your children are watching. Which shows might you watch with them? Which shows are inappropriate?

- Articulate clearly your TV watching policies in conjunction with your partner and any other caregivers (you can use the TV Policy Worksheet on my 52WeeksofParentingWisdom.com website). Like anything else, parenting partners must be on board with the policies so that they are enforced consistently.

- Share your policies with your children.

WEEK  48

Learn at the Library

Trips to the Library: Instill a love for books

As a child, I participated in our local library's summer reading program, in which I selected a book from one of the specified categories each week, met with the librarian to discuss it, and kept track of my progress on the library's summer reading chart. I particularly recall that I discovered genres and authors that I might not have otherwise chosen and enjoyed the challenge of finishing the recommended categories before the summer's end.

Most libraries still offer such summer programs, but you can also create your own reading club with your child during the summer or any other time, even if she is not yet reading. Selections for younger children will likely be picture books that you read to them; for older children, the books might be ones that they can read themselves or aloud to you, or more difficult books for you to read to them. If your child goes to sleep-away camp, you can each read the same books while she is gone, which is a great way to stay connected. A book club can help your children get excited about reading as they keep track of their progress, and they will also gain important skills in analyzing and comparing.

First, choose a theme for your current "club"—a genre, subject, series, or author that will allow for enough variety. If you have more than one child, the whole family can choose a theme that works with different age levels, or each child can have her own.

Here are some possible examples of themes for pre-readers:

- Stories about animals
- Fairy tales from around the world
- An author/illustrator, such as Eric Carle or Leo Lionni

For older children:

- A genre, such as science fiction, historical fiction, or mystery
- A series, such as American Girl or The Time Warp Trio (John Sczieska)
- A topic, such as sports (reading authors Mike Lupica and Dan Gutman)
- An author, such as Roald Dahl or Andrew Clements

One summer, my daughter and I read picture books based on East Asian folktales, including *Tikki-Tikki Tembo, The Five Chinese Brothers,* and *The Empty Pot.* As another example, for the good part of a year, my youngest son and I made our way through much of the *Magic Treehouse* series by Mary Pope Osborne.

Take a trip to the library and ask your librarian to recommend books that fit your theme, and once you are off and reading, create a chart with your child to keep track of your progress. If possible, enhance the experience with activities related to the topic, such as art projects, museum visits, and movies. For example, if you're reading animal stories, you could keep a list of all the creatures that appear in your selections and then take a trip to the zoo to see how many you can find. Keep it fun and light and see what ideas develop. Once you start, your child will lead the way.

QUESTIONS FOR REFLECTION

- What reading themes might my child/family enjoy? What genres and subjects do my children like and what new ones might they like to explore?

- Does our family take advantage of the public library to reinforce the idea that one can conserve and practice responsibility by borrowing books?

TO DO THIS WEEK

- Come up with a theme for a book club, soliciting your child's ideas if appropriate.

- Take a trip to the library. (Have your child sign up for a library card if possible.)

- Seek the help of the children's librarian to search out the best books within your theme.

- Set aside some time to read each day. Download the Book Club chart on the 52WeeksofParentingWisdom.com website to keep track of your reading activity.

WEEK  49

Toys R Not Always Us

Toys and Games: Choosing strategically

While I do believe in avoiding excess, I also think it's good to have an adequate supply of toys to keep kids stimulated. Don't base choices merely on convenience. Select toys that teach a variety of skills, including cooperation, strategy, probability, and memory.

Just as we often gravitate toward purchasing the same kind of clothing for ourselves repeatedly, we sometimes inadvertently choose toys for our children that are very similar to toys they already own. In order to keep your children engaged and foster their development, you should consider toys and games that encourage various kinds of play:

- Creative versus structured—Nurture both realms by owning some open-ended toys (e.g., dolls, blocks, art materials), as well as toys that have specific rules (e.g., games, puzzles).

- Number of participants—Have some toys for solitary play and some that your child can play with other children or grown-ups.

- Length of play—Include some that can be played in a short time and others that are appropriate for a longer game-playing session and require more focus.

Be very selective. Many mediocre toys and games are found in mainstream toy stores. I suggest that you resist:

- "Manipulatives" (blocks or snap-together components) that don't have enough pieces to keep a child challenged for more than a few minutes.

- Battery-operated toys. In addition to generally offering inferior playing and learning opportunities (including rote learning, which is next on this list), the fact that they break very easily and require frequent battery changes is highly annoying. (The only battery-operated toy I recommend is the electronic globe by LeapFrog.)

- Rote-learning toys. "Authentic" learning is more engaging and more effective than rote learning. For example, an interactive computer game that shows a child ten bananas and requires him to divide the bananas equally among five monkeys is better than a game that simply asks him to divide ten by five.

- Many well-known board games. They are often based mostly on chance and involve players progressing around a board by rolling dice, spinning a spinner, or popping a pop-o-matic. You and your children will lose interest in minutes. Good board games have something interesting happening on each turn and keep players engaged in strategizing or negotiating while others take their turn.

- Games that take more than an hour to play. Unless your children have an exceptionally long attention span, those games will collect dust in the closet.

The age guidelines on toys and games should certainly be followed to the extent they relate to possible choking hazards, but should otherwise be used only for general reference. Approriateness depends on your child's skills and ability to follow directions and focus. Carefully consider the specific skills needed to play with a given item (reading reviews is helpful) to determine if your child has the necessary skills or is ready to acquire them.

Choosing games is especially tricky when you have several children of widely different ages. Try to pick some games that will be especially good for each child and others that will be good for the whole family. Some games are "simple yet complex"—they are easy to learn with a few simple rules (so young children can play), but they also involve deep strategy, so older children and adult players are challenged. You can also seek out games that allow older children or adults to team up with younger children if a game is too difficult for a young child to play without assistance.

Keep your child's interests (dinosaurs, trains, fairies, baseball) in mind, but branch out so that not all your child's toys center around one theme. You want to open up new worlds for your child.

Avoid board games based on TV shows or movies; I have yet to see a good one. Whether it's the Little Mermaid—3-D Under The Sea Adventure or Raiders of the Lost Ark game, you can be sure that the tie-in will be contrived and the playing mode will be dull and based mostly on chance. And try not to make an impulse purchase. It usually results in a toy that your child plays with for a week (or maybe just a day) and then forgets.

Because playing is one of the main vehicles for learning, choosing your child's toys and games carefully is a more important piece of the parenting puzzle than you might think.

QUESTIONS FOR REFLECTION

- Do my children quickly lose interest in the toys and games we buy them?

- Do we have a large number of toys collecting dust on the shelf?

- Do I give careful thought to the toy purchases I make, or are many of our selections impulse purchases that end up being disappointments?

TO DO THIS WEEK

- Give away toys and games that are uninteresting or that your child has outgrown.

- Check out teacher supply stores and online educational toy companies; they have the best selection of learning toys and creative games. Use the above guidelines to make informed selections.

- For suggestions of excellent toys and games and where to purchase them, see 52WeeksofParentingWisdom.com.

WEEK  50

Constructive Computer Time

Computer Activities: Some are excellent for young children (but many aren't)

I know many parents who don't let their kids use computers until they are school age or even older. I respect this decision, but my philosophy is that if appropriate games and programs are used in the right way—with reasonable boundaries and not to the exclusion of other play and learning media—computers are OK at almost any age. Indeed, computer time can be not just fun and instructive, but can contribute to family connectedness.

I avoid computer programs that teach by rote (such as the *Reader Rabbit* series)—you might as well just give your child vocabulary or spelling quizzes. Rather, I look for games that capitalize on the power of computers by altering scenarios depending on your child's input. Computer games can teach dexterity, logic and problem solving, resource management, and many other skills.

Look for games that the adults will enjoy playing with their children (this allows computer games to become familiy activities). That means games that offer gradations of difficulty. Zoo Tycoon is a good example. In this game the player builds a zoo, which earns money depending on what animals are on display, how they are cared for, and what amenities the "keeper" provides. A very young child can easily become proficient in an

191

hour or so, but the more sophisticated aspects of the game will challenge older children and adults. At all ages, creating and managing a zoo provides an engaging opportunity for enjoyable learning and interaction.

You must set boundaries regarding the use of technology (and media) and monitor the time spent on any one particular activity (see Week 47: *Is TV Bad?*). But, if you choose computer games carefully and incorporate them thoughtfully, they can become a very positive part of your family life.

QUESTIONS FOR REFLECTION

- How much time do my children spend playing computer games?

- Do I select computer games carefully, looking for nonviolent and educational games that make the most of new technology?

- Do I interact with my children and computer games together?

TO DO THIS WEEK

- If you already let your children play computer games, take a close look at how they spend their time in front of the screen. What are the benefits of the games they are playing, other than filling time? Eliminate games that aren't challenging or instructive and that don't support your values.

- Seek out several good computer games or websites; do the research when your children are asleep or away.

- Set boundaries for computer time and share the rules with your children.

- Make sure that some of the time your children spend with computer games is also spent with you.

WEEK  51

My Favorite Things

Individuality: Find out how well you know your child

Most parents think they know their children well. After all, we are responsible for them 24/7 and (hopefully) spend much of our waking hours together. I'm often surprised when I ask parents a question such as "What does your child enjoy doing most?" or "What's your child's favorite book?" and, amazingly, some parents can't answer. We can get bogged down in the day-to-day drudgery of parenting and sometimes forget that, in the end, it's all about raising happy, healthy kids. Only by knowing his likes (and dislikes) can you make appropriate choices for your child and let him know that his preferences matter to you.

If you don't feel you really know what makes your child happy, here's an exercise: Make a list of things you think your child most enjoys (books, games, foods, and so on). Then, ask your child to list some of his favorite things. See how much overlap there is between the lists.

Starting Early

If your child is too young for this exercise, try to answer the following list of questions yourself:

What's my baby's favorite _____?

- Food?
- Toy?
- Story?
- Song?

As They Grow

For older children, you can add more complex questions, such as:

- If you were going to be on a desert island for a year, what five things, aside from food, would you bring with you to keep yourself entertained?

- If we could go anywhere on a family vacation, where would you choose?

- What is your favorite holiday? Why?

- What's your greatest pet peeve?

- What person outside of your family members do you admire the most? Why?

- Which would you most like to win: An Oscar for best actor? An Olympic Medal? A Presidential Election? The Nobel Peace Prize?

QUESTIONS FOR REFLECTION

• How difficult is it for me to list the specific things my child enjoys?

TO DO THIS WEEK

• Do the above exercise with each of your children this week. If you discover that you know your children very well, you can relax this week! If not, you might want to review Week 17.

WEEK  52

Great Parents Are Made, Not Born

The Parenting Journey: Continue to improve your parenting skills

When I began my career as a parenting educator, I read an article about the rise in "outsourcing" of parental functions. The article criticized parents who hired people to baby-proof their homes or teach their child to ride a bike. The writer went on to bemoan the fact that this trend demonstrates that parents no longer trust their natural parenting instincts.

On the one hand, I agreed with the author that a parent should parent. On the other hand, I was annoyed that the writer confused two different ideas: shirking parental duties and seeking support. Hiring someone to toilet train your child isn't appropriate, but asking for advice on toilet training is.

I know I'm preaching to the choir here because unless you just picked up this book and skipped to the last chapter to see how it ends, you've been engaged in the process of improving your parenting skills. Clearly you believe in parenting education. But I want to share my philosophy about parenting education in order to encourage you to *continue*.

Society accepts the idea of people seeking advice and instruction, even regarding "natural" activities—we exercise naturally, but we hire trainers; we make homes naturally, but we hire decorators. Why should parenting, which is one of the most important roles one can have in life, be any different? Don't get me wrong; I'm a big believer in the importance of paying attention to one's instincts. But what happens when the thing our instincts tell us to do isn't working?

> I'm a big believer in the importance of paying attention to one's instincts. But what happens when the thing our instincts tell us to do isn't working?

When my first child was born, I fell fairly easily into my mothering role and was fortunate to share parenting responsibilities with my husband, who was comfortable in his role as a father. We also had the baby's grandparents for support and terrific role models. Despite all these factors in my favor, I still had countless moments when I felt at best unsure, and at worst downright inept. I needed advice and found it when I sought wisdom from those with experience, attended workshops, read, and shared struggles with other new moms in my mothers' group. The more I sought opportunities to learn and the more I combined my gained knowledge with my gut instinct, the more assuredly and intentionally I made parenting decisions.

Information and guidance are tools that will go a long, long way in helping you parent intentionally, so avail yourself of as many resources as you can. You're not "outsourcing;" you're working to become a more successful parent.

Remember, as philosopher George Santayana said, "The wisest mind has something yet to learn."

QUESTIONS FOR REFLECTION

- In what areas do I feel most confident as a parent?

- What are the most significant positive changes I have made in my parenting in the past year?

- What changes have I seen in my children as a result?

- What areas could still use improvement?

TO DO THIS WEEK

- Review the Contents page of this book and see if there are sections you might want to reread.

- Make a list of the strengths and skills you've learned as a parent as a result of your *52 Weeks of Parenting Wisdom* experience.

- Decide what your next step is in your parenting journey. Do you want to join a parenting group? Read more about a specific topic? Attend parenting workshops?

MEG AKABAS

Meg Akabas is the founder of New York City-based Parenting Solutions™, a consultancy designed to help parents discover the joy in parenting. She regularly provides one-on-one consultations and leads workshops for parents and teachers on infancy through pre-adolescence. Meg has served as president of the board of two Manhattan schools and has more than 18 years of leadership experience in nursery and elementary schools. She has been awarded the "Parenting Educator Credential" from the New York State Parenting Education Partnership and serves on the NYSPEP steering committee. Meg lives with her husband, Seth, in Manhattan, where they have raised their four children. For more, visit www. parenting-solutions.com.

SETH AKABAS

Seth Akabas is a lawyer and Meg's faithful parenting and writing partner.